THE HOUSE.

HAND-BOOKS BY THE SAME AUTHOR.

EDUCATIONAL.

HOW TO WRITE: A New Pocket Manual of Composition and Letter Writing, with Hints on Penmanship and Writing Materials, and Practical Rules for Literary Composition, Newspaper Writing, Punctuation, and Proof Correcting, etc., etc. Price, post-paid, paper, 30 c.; cloth, 50 c.

HOW TO TALK: A New Pocket Manual of Conversation and Debate, with Directions for Acquiring a Grammatical and Graceful Style and more than Five Hundred Common Mistakes Corrected.
Price, paper, 30 c.; cloth, 50 cents.

HOW TO BEHAVE: A New Pocket Manual of Republican Etiquette, and Guide to Correct Personal Habits; with Rules for Debating Societies and Deliberative Assemblies, etc. Price, paper, 30 c.; cloth, 50 cts.

HOW TO DO BUSINESS: A New Pocket Manual of Practical Affairs and Guide to Success in Life; with a Collection of Business Forms, and a Dictionary of Commercial Terms, etc. Price, paper, 30 c.; cloth, 50 cents.

RURAL.

THE HOUSE: A New Pocket Manual of Rural Architecture; or, How to Build Dwellings, Barns, Stables, and Out Dwellings of all kinds. With a Chapter on Churches and School-Houses.
Price, post-paid, paper, 30 c.; muslin, 50 cents.

THE GARDEN: A New Pocket Manual of Practical Horticulture; or, How to Cultivate Vegetables, Fruits, and Flowers. With a Chapter on Ornamental Trees and Shrubs. Price, paper, 30 c.; cloth, 50 cents.

THE FARM: A New Pocket Manual of Practical Agriculture; or, How to Cultivate all the Field Crops. With an Essay on Farm Management, etc. Price, paper, 30 c.; muslin, 50 cents.

DOMESTIC ANIMALS: A New Pocket Manual of Cattle, Horse, and Sheep Husbandry; or, How to Breed and Rear the Various Tenants of the Barn-yard, etc., etc. Price, paper, 30 c.; cloth, 50 cents.

In Preparation.

THE RIGHT WORD IN THE RIGHT PLACE: A Pocket Dictionary of Synonyms, Technical Terms, Abbreviations, Foreign Phrases, etc., etc. With a Chapter on Punctuation and Proof Reading. Price, ; muslin, 50 cents.

RURAL MANUALS—No. 1.

THE HOUSE:

A POCKET MANUAL

OF

Rural Architecture:

OR, HOW TO BUILD

COUNTRY HOUSES AND OUT-BUILDINGS;

EMBRACING

THE ORIGIN AND MEANING OF THE HOUSE; THE ART OF HOUSE-BUILDING, INCLUDING PLANNING, STYLE, AND CONSTRUCTION; DESIGNS AND DESCRIPTIONS OF COTTAGES, FARM-HOUSES, VILLAS, AND OUT-BUILDINGS, OF VARIOUS COST AND IN THE DIFFERENT STYLES OF ARCHITECTURE, ETC., ETC.; AND AN APPENDIX, CONTAINING RECIPES FOR PAINTS AND WASHES, STUCCO, ROUGH-CAST, ETC.; AND INSTRUCTIONS FOR ROOFING, BUILDING WITH ROUGH STONE, UNBURNT BRICK, BALLOON FRAMES, AND THE CONCRETE OR GRAVEL WALL.

With Numerous Original Plans,

DESIGNED BY F. E. GRAEF, ARCHITECT, AND OTHERS.

BY THE AUTHOR OF "THE GARDEN," "THE FARM," ETC.

Until common sense finds its way into architecture, there can be little hope for it.—RUSKIN.

New York:
FOWLER AND WELLS, PUBLISHERS,
No. 308 BROADWAY.
1859.

DAVIES AND ROBERTS, Stereotypers,
113 Nassau Street, New York.

PREFACE.

In this country everybody builds a house—perhaps several of them. Everybody, then, should know something about domestic architecture, in order to build to the best advantage—to secure the largest amount of convenience, comfort, and beauty in his dwelling which his means and materials will permit. It has been our object, in the preparation of this manual, to promote the diffusion of this needed knowledge among the people.

The works of the lamented Downing, with all their acknowledged imperfections, have done much to enlighten the understandings and improve the tastes of our people on this subject. Much of the improvement which has taken place in the rural architecture of this country, within the last fifteen years, is due to their influence. But their size and cost have been a bar to their circulation, and confined their direct action upon the public mind within a comparatively narrow circle. The same remark will apply with more or less force to the excellent works of Calvert Vaux, Wheeler, Cleveland and Backus Brothers, and other recent architectural writers.

We have aimed here at a wider, if not a stronger, influence. We have condensed into this little volume all that the great majority of readers will care to find in it, and all that they are prepared to appreciate and profit by; and have placed the whole within the reach of every man in America who will ever have occasion to erect a house, a barn, a stable, or a piggery, by placing it at a price which no one will be too poor to pay. We aim, by these means, at a universal circulation and almost unlimited usefulness.

The plan and execution of our work will speak for themselves. We are fully aware of its imperfections, some of which, being accidental and inseparable from a first edition, will be hereafter obviated. In the mean time, a generous public will not allow them to blind their eyes to the merits which it will, we trust, be acknowledged to possess. We leave it, with full confidence, in their hands.

In the department of design we have been aided throughout by Mr. John Crumly, a competent and reliable architect of this city, whom we take this occasion to recommend to our readers.

We are also largely indebted to Mr. F. E. Graef, Architect, 56 Wall Street, New York, whose designs, duly credited in the body of the work, will not fail to command general approval for their beauty and perfect adaptation to their purpose. Mr. Graef is a man of practical knowledge, good sense, and executive ability, as well as a thoroughly educated and skillful artist (being a graduate of the Prussian Academy in Berlin), and will, we feel sure, give entire satisfaction to any of our patrons who may employ him.

CONTENTS.

I.—ORIGIN AND MEANING OF THE HOUSE.

II.—HOUSE-BUILDING.

III.—COTTAGES OF ONE STORY.

IV.—STORY-AND-A-HALF COTTAGES.

V.—HOUSES OF TWO STORIES.

VI.—FARM-HOUSES.

VII.—VILLAS.

VIII.—BARNS, AND OTHER OUT-BUILDINGS.

IX.—CHURCHES AND SCHOOL-HOUSES.

APPENDIX.

THE HOUSE.

I.

ORIGIN AND MEANING OF THE HOUSE.

Much of the character of every man may be read in his house.—*Downing.*

I.—THE WIGWAM AND THE TENT.

S "the groves were God's first temples," so, undoubtedly, were they the earliest dwellings of man. The dense foliage of the trees afforded protection against the too fervid rays of the noonday sun, and their hollow trunks, and the caves among the rocks which they overhung, served as a shelter from the fury of the storm. By twining together the tops of saplings growing near each other, and filling in the spaces between them with branches broken from other trees, arbors or bough-houses were readily constructed. These, in the Eden-like climates of the East, where the race is supposed to have originated, probably satisfied the wants of the men of the first ages.

At a later day, and in a less genial climate, dwellings were constructed by cutting down trees and placing them, in a circular form, with their tops leaning against each other and fastening them together, branches being interwoven and the interstices filled with clay. Of this description is the wigwam of

the North American savage. In other cases a frame-work of poles was covered with strips of bark or skins of animals. The dome-like mud huts of some of the African tribes, with holes two or three feet high for doors, through which one must enter "on all-fours," advance in point of architecture one step further.

Out of the necessities of a pastoral life grew the invention of tents, which were at first made of the skins of animals and afterward of felt and various kinds of cloth. On each green and chosen spot these portable habitations could be spread in a moment, and as readily removed. Even at the present day,

> The Arab band,
> Across the sand,
> Still bear their dwellings light,
> And 'neath the skies
> Their tents arise,
> Like spirits of the night.

II.—THE LOG CABIN.

The inventor of the rectangular log-house should have been immortalized; but, alas! he is unknown, and the date of the

Fig. 1.—The Ancient Log Cabin.

first dwelling of this kind is nowhere recorded. However long ago that event may have occurred, the foundations of the art of domestic architecture were then securely established. The first oblong house, covered by a sloping roof, whether its walls were constructed of logs placed horizontally one above the other, in the American backwoods style, or of upright posts, as shown in the foregoing engraving, contained the germ of the cottage, the mansion, and the villa of to-day.

III.—THE SAXON HALL.

Speaking of the Saxons, Turner, in his "Early History of Domestic Architecture in England," says:

"Without mechanical skill to work the quarries made by the Romans, and while the habitations of the mass of the people were mud or wooden huts of one room only, in the middle of which the fire was kindled, the Saxon *thegne* built his hall from the woods of his *demesne* by the labor of his bondsmen. It was thatched with straw or reeds or roofed with wooden shingles. Its plan was little more than its name implied—a capacious apartment, which in the daytime was adapted to the patriarchal hospitality of the owner, and formed at night a sort of stable for his servants, to whose rude accommodation their master's was not much superior in an adjoining chamber. The fire was kindled in the center of the hall, the smoke making its way out through an opening in the roof immediately above the hearth, or by the door, windows, and eaves of thatch. The lord and his 'hearthmen'—a significant appellation given to his most familiar retainers—sat by the same fire at which their repast was cooked, and at night retired to share the same dormitory, which served them also as a council chamber."

The Normans introduced little change in the general plans of dwellings, the chief room and single bedchamber still prevailing, even in regal residences. It was in details chiefly that architectural novelties betokened French influence. Chimneys were generally unknown till the fifteenth century, although a few examples occur earlier. Shutters and canvas, instead of glazed windows, continued in general use in dwelling-houses to the reign of Henry III., notwithstanding painted glass for church windows was not uncommon in the twelfth century.

Of the castles, monasteries, and moated granges of a later day it is not necessary to speak. Their general forms are made familiar to all by means of pictures and engravings of all descriptions, scattered through our picture-galleries and books. The manor-house and the villa of the sixteenth and seventeenth centuries form the basis of many a modern design.

IV.—SIGNIFICANCE OF THE HOUSE.

We have hinted at, rather than described, some of the changes through which the dwelling-house has reached its present external form and internal arrangement; but our brief statement will serve to indicate the fact, that each change has resulted from a corresponding change in the habits, wants, and tastes of the builder. The house of each epoch forms a chapter in the world's history. In the wigwam of the savage we recognize an expression of the rude life of the forest-born hunter, lacking the refinement which would require, as well as the skill which might provide, anything beyond a mere shelter. The tents of the nomadic tribes are not less significant of their habits and modes of existence—

> While on from plain to plain they led their flocks,
> In search of clearer spring and fresher field.

So have the log cabin, the hall of the Saxon *thegne*, the feudal castle, the monastery, the grange, the manor-house, the cottage, and the villa, their readily comprehended meanings. Each was called into existence by the exigences of the social period to which it belongs, and reveals the principal features in the life of its first inhabitants.

"The different styles of domestic architecture," as Downing truly remarks, "the Roman, the Italian, the Swiss, the Venetian, the Rural Gothic, are nothing more than expressions of national character which have, through long use, become permanent. Thus the gay and sunny temperament of the south of

Europe is well expressed in the light balconies, the grouped windows, the open arcades, and the statue and vase bordered terraces of the Venetian and Italian villas; the homely yet strong and quaint character of the Swiss in their broad-roofed, half rude, and curiously constructed cottages; the domestic virtues and the love of rural beauty and seclusion can not possibly be better expressed than in the English cottage, with its many upward pointing gables, its intricate tracery, its spacious bay windows, and its walls covered with vines and flowering shrubs."

Domestic architecture is not only capable of expressing the characters and customs of nations and epochs; individual diversities of opinion, feeling, taste, and modes of life may be and are also clearly embodied in the human dwelling. Mere utilitarianism expresses itself in a square or oblong box-like house, with walls and roof built only to defend the inmates against cold and heat; windows intended for nothing but to admit the light and exclude the air; and chimneys constructed only to carry off the smoke. A love of ornament and show, unguided by either sound judgment or cultivated taste, give us all sorts of absurd and incongruous combinations of styles; build cottages in the form of villas and villas like castles of the middle ages; and set all the laws of fitness and order at defiance. Good sense, a true love of the beautiful, refinement, culture, and domestic habits are equally sure, under favorable circumstances, to make their impress upon the walls of the dwelling-house. Hospitality smiles in ample parlors; home virtues dwell in cosy fireside family rooms; intellectuality is seen in well-stocked libraries, and a dignified love of leisure and repose in cool and spacious verandas.

Much of the character of every man, it is truly said, may be read in his house. If he has molded its leading features from the foundation, it will give a clew to a large part of his character. If he has taken it from the hands of another, it will, in its internal details and use, show at a glance something of the daily thoughts and life of the family that inhabits it.

II.

HOUSE-BUILDING.

He who improves the dwellings of a people, in relation to their comforts, habits, and morals, makes a benignant and lasting reform at the very foundations of society.—*Village and Farm Cottages.*

I.—FUNDAMENTAL PRINCIPLES.

HAVING traced the dwelling-house to its origin, and pointed out the significance of its various forms, we shall now, before presenting the designs and descriptions which form the main body of our work, proceed to lay before the reader a few practical hints and suggestions on the general subject of house-building. These hints and suggestions will necessarily be briefly expressed; but their importance must not be measured by the space they occupy.

We have little to do here with the theory of architecture; but there are two or three fundamental principles involved in house-building which we wish, at the outset, distinctly to impress upon the reader's mind.

1. *Adaptation to Use.*—In erecting a building of any kind, the first thing to be considered, and the last to be lost sight of, is the *use* to which it is to be appropriated. Adaptation to this use must not be sacrificed to anything else. The plan and construction of a dwelling-house, for instance, must be quite different from those of a church edifice or a barn; because its purpose and uses are different. For the same reason, a country residence should not resemble a city dwelling, and a farm-

house should be unlike the cottage of the mechanic. And the law of fitness applies to all the details of a house as well as to its general form. It should be our guide in the arrangement of rooms; in the disposition of doors, windows, stairs, and chimneys; and in the provisions made for warming and ventilation. Adaptation to climate, situation, and the condition and means of the proprietor falls under the same head. Let it be remembered, then, that *this principle of fitness, or adaptation to use, lies at the foundation of all satisfactory house-building.* It will be more fully illustrated as we proceed.

2. *Expression of Purpose.*—But it is not enough that a building be planned with strict reference to the uses to which it is to be devoted. Truthfulness, which should run through all our works, as well as our words, demands that its purpose shall be expressed in its construction—that a church, for instance, shall not require a label to inform us of its ecclesiastic character, and that a dwelling-house shall be known as such at a glance. This principle, strange as it may seem, is frequently violated. Church edifices are made to look like barns, dwelling-houses are built on the model of a Grecian temple, and we sometimes see stables which may be mistaken, at the first glance, for farm cottages.

"The prominent features conveying expression of purpose in dwelling-houses," Downing says, "are the chimneys, the windows, and the porch, veranda, or piazza; and for this reason, whenever it is desired to raise the character of a cottage or a villa above mediocrity, attention should be first bestowed on those portions of the building." Loudon says: "In every human habitation the chimney-tops should be conspicuous objects, because they are its essential characteristics. They distinguish apartments destined for human beings from those designed for lodging cattle." First, then, build *fitting* habitations for yourself and family; and, second, *let this fitness be clearly expressed in their external features.*

3. *Manifestation of Beauty.*—A house may be strictly adapted to its uses and clearly express its purpose, and yet be a

very unsatisfactory dwelling for a person of taste and culture, and a perpetual blemish in the landscape. It may have comfortable rooms, well distributed in relation to each other and their uses; windows, doors, chimneys, etc., of the proper size and in their proper places; and air, water, and warmth well provided for, and yet make a very unsatisfactory impression. The sentiment of beauty may find no expression in it. The windows may be mere holes in the wall, closed by glazed sashes, and the chimneys unsightly heaps of brick. This lack of all sentiment—this devotion to mere literal utility—is too frequently displayed in rural house-building in this country. It will disappear as taste and culture advance, and the love of the beautiful, inherent in every man and woman, is called out and developed. Let the reader bear in mind, then, the fact, that every house, however humble, should and may be characterized by these three qualities—

1. Adaptation to Use;
2. Expression of Purpose; and,
3. Manifestation of Beauty.

II.—CHOICE OF A SITE.

In selecting a site for a country house, many circumstances should be taken into consideration. First among these, in point of importance, is

1. *Healthfulness.*—No combination of advantages can compensate the lack of a salubrious atmosphere. Such a defect, unless its causes come clearly within the purchaser's control, should be considered fatal. The vicinity of stagnant swamps and marshes; the borders of sluggish streams; and all situations where the soil is too retentive of moisture and can not be easily and thoroughly drained, should be carefully avoided. A house in such a situation is no less uncomfortable than unhealthful, being continually damp and chilly.

Elevated grounds in the immediate vicinity of extensive swamps and marshes, especially if in the direction of prevailing winds, are liable to be quite as much affected by the malarious air as the low grounds themselves, and should be shunned for the same reason.

Next in importance to good air is pure water; and one should never adopt a site for a dwelling-house without having satisfied himself that an abundant supply of this essential element can be readily procured. The importance of this point, in its bearings upon health and comfort, are sadly underrated by the great majority of our people. It should be universally known that many serious and dangerous diseases may be traced to the use of impure water. In regions where the water is universally "hard" or limy, rain water properly filtered should be used for drinking and cooking, as well as for washing.

2. *Convenience of Access.*—In many cases nearness to one's place of business, or to the railway station or steamboat landing, has naturally considerable influence in determining the choice of a lot. This circumstance should not, however, have too much weight. An additional quarter of a mile added to the tri-daily walk of a man of sedentary employments may be an advantage rather than otherwise; and often a much better site can be obtained for the same amount of money by foregoing the slight advantages of a more central locality.

Where mere business motives may be left out of the account, the tastes and habits of the family will have a controlling influence. One will seek the frequented street or highway, while another will choose a quiet lane or an out-of-the-way nook.

It is not necessary, as many seem to suppose, that a farm-house or the residence of a man of leisure should be close to the highway. A sufficient distance from it to avoid the noise and dust, and secure privacy and quiet, is far preferable; but at the same time, unless one desires to cut himself off from all intercourse with the world, his house should be easy of access.

3. *Suitableness of Ground.*—The cost of building, digging cellars and wells, etc., is greatly influenced by the nature of the ground, which must, therefore, always enter into the account. It sometimes costs more to prepare the grounds for building

than to build the house. This is well enough when advantages are secured which really warrant the outlay; but the circumstance should have its due weight in determining one's choice.

The adaptation of the surrounding soil to the purpose of culture and the growth of trees may be considered under the same head. A good garden plot in the vicinity of the house is very desirable, but we find little soil in this country that may not easily be brought to the desired state of fertility, although originally what is called poor.

4. *Altitude.*—A somewhat elevated site has many advantages—beauty of prospect, salubrity and dryness of air, facilities for drainage, etc.—but is generally comparatively difficult of access, and unless sheltered on the north and west by higher grounds or by belts of trees, bleak and uncomfortable in winter. Some valleys, however, are equally bleak, the wind sweeping through them with a power unknown even on the hill-top. Loudon says, that of all varieties of hilly surface, the most desirable site is where a prominent knoll stands forward from a lengthened ridge, and where the latter has a valley with a river in front and higher hills rising one above another behind. One of the worst sites is the steep uniform side of a hill, closely surrounded by other hills equally high and steep.

The style of building you propose to erect (if first decided upon) must be considered with reference to this point. A plain, low cottage very properly nestles in some quiet nook at the base of a hill or ridge, while the more pretending ornamental villa may with equal propriety crown its summit.

5. *Aspect.*—The choice of an aspect should be determined mainly by local and climatic considerations; a free play for the cooling breeze being essential in one place, and a shelter from wintry winds exceedingly desirable in another. In all climates we should, if possible, secure a barrier either of higher grounds or thick belts of trees (evergreens are best) on the side of the house looking in the direction from which violent storms most frequently come. The north side of a high hill or ridge, where

the direct rays of the sun would be excluded for a large portion of the time, is entirely unfit for a building site, sunlight being everywhere essential to health and comfort. In a northern climate, a southern or southeastern exposure with sheltering hills on the north is generally preferred.

In reference to the main points from which it is seen, and the avenues by which it is approached, a house should be so placed, if practicable, as to present an agreeable appearance, being neither too closely screened nor too much exposed.

6. *Trees, etc.*—A grove or belt of well-grown forest trees, to serve as a shelter and a basis for future operations in planting, adds greatly to the value of a site; indeed, so important do we consider this point, that we should make it an essential one in our own case. But such situations are not always readily found, and some would, doubtless, prefer to plant their own trees, even when they can not hope to live long enough to see them in their fully developed beauty.

There are many other objects which it is desirable to include in one's grounds, when practicable, without sacrificing other and more important considerations, such as a clear running stream, a sheet of water in repose, a picturesque ledge of rock, a shaded, naiad-haunted ravine, etc.; but these are not generally included in a village lot, and do not come within the reach of all. Let each secure whatever of beauty and comfort he can in his house and its surroundings, and "learn therewith to be content."

III.—ADOPTION OF A PLAN.

No man should commence the erection of even the smallest cottage without having previously adopted a well digested and fully matured plan. It is not enough that he may have a general idea of the form and size of the building he purposes to erect. All the details of its internal arrangement—the size and situation of the various rooms, halls, closets, pantry, etc., and the exact place of stairs, chimneys, doors, and windows, should all be determined before the first stake is driven to mark its outlines upon the ground. If this course be not adopted, serious and expensive mistakes are almost sure to be made, and money wasted in needless alterations. If you do not know what you want, you are not prepared to build, and should wait till your necessities and tastes have assumed definite forms. While your house is yet only a paper cottage or villa it may easily be changed to meet your changing whims; but when your thought has once shaped itself in brick and mortar, it has become a matter of enduring record. See to it that it be such a record as you are willing should be read by posterity.

Adopt no plan hastily, whether conceived by yourself or offered by another. It should be carefully studied, examined in every light, looked at from every point of view. There are many things to be taken into consideration.

1. In the first place, your house must be adapted to the site you have chosen. A plan may be admirable in itself, and yet unsuited to a particular spot. It must be looked at, then, in reference to the ground it is to occupy; or if the plan be adopted first, the site must be selected in accordance with it. Not merely the style and general character of a house are influenced by the contour and aspect of the features of the landscape around, but its outlines upon the ground, its arrangement in masses, is equally subject to the great law of fitness.*

2. If one's pecuniary resources are limited, the amount of money which he can appropriate to building will greatly influence the character of his plan. Reception-rooms, drawing-rooms, libraries, boudoirs, and so on, are certainly desirable; but if you have but seven or eight hundred dollars to expend in building, it would be folly to put them all into your plan. You must be content with a small number of rooms, making, if necessary, several of them serve two or three distinct uses.

Consider first what accommodations are absolutely essential to your comfort, and then what appliances of convenience or luxury you can add. Do not plan too largely. Depend upon

* Gervase Wheeler.

it, you will enjoy a much larger sum of happiness in a small house wholly paid for, than in a large one which has involved you in debt.

3. Having decided what sort of a house is best adapted to your site, and what amount of accommodations the sum you purpose to appropriate will secure, consider next how you can make that amount of accommodation best subserve the particular wants and tastes of yourself and family. No two households are exactly alike in their domestic habits, and a house which your neighbor Brown finds "just the thing," would require considerable modification probably to adapt it to your purpose; so in making a plan, or in studying those which we offer in this work, with a view to the adoption of one of them, keep the requirements of your particular household constantly in view, and adopt, modify, or reject accordingly, remembering that the first grand requirement of every dwelling-house is *fitness* or adaptation to its uses.

The fact that individual wants and tastes are infinitely varied, renders it impossible for us to give either directions or plans that will exactly suit individual cases; but we will here briefly advert to some general principles which should govern in the development or choice of a plan.

1. *General Form.*—The largest space in proportion to the extent of the wall may be included in the circular form, but, although round houses have been built, as we shall show further on, this shape is not a desirable one. The octagon approaches the circle in shape and in economy of outside wall. This form is, in our view, open to serious objections, but to give our readers an opportunity to judge for themselves in reference to its advantages and disadvantages, we give plans of octagon houses in another chapter.

O. S. Fowler, in his "Home for All,"* has advocated this form with an earnestness which could only come from thorough conviction of its superiority over all others. To that work we

---

* Published by Fowler and Wells; price, 87 cents.

must refer those who may desire to see what can be said in its favor.

Of the common forms adopted in house-building, the square is the most economical in point of outside wall, and allows the most compact arrangement of rooms. Many prefer it to all others. A square house can not easily be made picturesque, but need not be, as such houses too often are, a mere characterless box. The advantages of the winged form, in its various modifications, are a more perfect adaptation to the high-pitched roof, greater picturesqueness, and more varied aspects. One part can also often be so projected as to shelter another and more important one from prevailing winds and storms.

2. *Aspect.*—With regard to the aspect of a dwelling-house, and the disposition of its various rooms in reference to the points of compass, the principal objects to be kept in view are: 1. Shelter from prevailing winds and storms; 2. Enjoyment of particular views afforded by the situation; 3. Exposure to or protection from the sun. In cold and temperate climates a southern or southwestern exposure is most desirable for the principal rooms. In the Northern and Middle States generally, a northeastern aspect is, if possible, to be avoided, our most disagreeable storms coming from that quarter. In hot climates, a northern exposure is sometimes chosen on account of its coolness.

3. *Arrangement of Rooms.*—But other considerations besides those mentioned in the preceding section should of course have an influence in deciding the disposition of the various apartments of a dwelling. The convenience of the house as a whole must not be sacrificed to promote the comfort of a single apartment. The end to be secured is the most perfect adaptation possible of the entire structure to the purpose for which it is erected. This purpose, in its details, being almost infinitely varied, of course the arrangement of rooms, in common with the architectural features, mode of construction, etc., will vary accordingly, no two families requiring precisely the same accommodations. We can only offer a few hints for general appli-

cation. Our ideas on this point, together with those of other persons, will be found elaborated in the plans presented in other chapters.

Having utility constantly in view, labor-saving must be made a prominent idea in our arrangement of rooms. This is necessary in the habitations of the rich as well as of the poor. The difficulty of getting good servants, and the cares and vexations attending the employment of bad or indifferent ones, render it desirable for even the wealthy to employ as few of them as possible. To promote the saving of labor, and convenience in performing the domestic labors of a household, we should study compactness, avoiding, so far as other important considerations will permit, extended wings and long passages. The rooms, too, most closely related in their uses should be brought near each other; the dining-room, for instance, being so placed as to afford easy ingress and egress from the kitchen, while at the same time it is desirable that the one should not open directly into the other. To the same end, a pantry, sink-room, closets, etc., should be provided for in connection with the dining-room and kitchen. When there is a basement, some will prefer to place the kitchen and its offices in that, and the dining-room on the principal floor. This is a more elegant but a less convenient arrangement than having them on the same floor. A dumb waiter, however, will obviate, in part at least, the objections to this plan. The entrance hall should generally be central in position, and if possible furnish access to every room on the first floor. In some plans, however, in order to economize space, it is advisable to deviate from this rule. It should open toward the south, east, or west, if possible, and not toward the north.

When it is practicable, there should be at least one room on the first floor provided with the means of warmth and ventilation, which can be used as a sleeping-room in case of sickness or other need.

The duties of hospitality should not be neglected, and provision must be made, in every plan which will admit it, for spare chambers, a parlor, etc.; we do not, however, or at least we should not, build our houses for our guests, but for ourselves and families, and we protest against the sacrifice of family convenience and home-comfort, often made, for the purpose of entertaining occasional visitors more elegantly. Would it not be well for our very utilitarian people to consider whether it really "pays" to provide an elegant and comfortable parlor—perhaps the only handsome room in the house—to be used, as is the case in many country dwellings, scarcely a dozen times in a year? Take our advice, and if you have a peculiarly handsome, agreeable, and comfortable room in your house, whether it be called parlor, saloon, or drawing-room, furnish and adorn it in the best manner your means will permit, and then *use* it—avail yourself of its benefits by throwing it open for daily family occupancy; and when guests arrive, welcome them also to all its advantages. They will feel much more at home there than in a room which has been opened on their arrival for the first time in a month or two.

Sleeping apartments should be of good size, well-lighted, and well-ventilated, and each should have separate means of access to a hall, corridor, or passage. Their distribution will generally be suggested by that of the rooms below.

Every house should have a bath-room. In assigning it its place, reference should be had to ease of access, facility of conveying water, and security against damage from any accidental leakage. A water-closet, either in connection with the bathing-room or in some other convenient situation, is very desirable, and should be provided for wherever the pecuniary means at the command of the builder will permit.

4. *Miscellaneous Hints.*—A pantry convenient to the dining-room, and if practicable opening from it, should be provided for in every house. A sink-room and closets must be thought of in the same connection. Every sleeping room should also have a closet if practicable; but we would not sacrifice the proportion and beauty of a room by cutting off closets where they can not conveniently be made without violence to the design.

The situation of the chimneys should be made the subject of careful consideration. They give most warmth when placed in the inner walls, but in some styles of building are more picturesque on the exterior.

Stairs should generally be central in position, broad, and not too high. A back door should be provided, both for convenience and for the purpose of ventilation, of which more anon. Windows on opposite sides of a room are generally to be avoided, on account of their unpleasant "cross lights."

IV.—STYLE OF ARCHITECTURE.

The domestic architecture of a people should be the natural outgrowth of its character, institutions, customs, and habits, modified by the climate and scenery in the midst of which it is built up. In this way originated the English cottage, the Swiss *chalêt*, and the Italian villa. Having in this country institutions differing from those of any other, together with many peculiarities of character, habits, and climate, we can not consistently adopt in full the architecture of any other people or country. We should have a style, or perhaps several styles, peculiar to ourselves; and no doubt we shall have them in due time. Thus far we have been content to build in every style, ancient and modern, and, most of all, in *no* style; covering the whole face of the country with incongruous and unsightly structures. There are various causes for this state of things, the principal of which are the necessary devotion of our people to the rough work of subduing a new country; the consequent lack of thought and culture in the right direction; and the want of true home-feeling, growing out of our migratory habits. These causes are becoming year by year less operative, and our domestic architecture is improving in the same ratio—exceptions to the general ugliness of our buildings growing more and more numerous as leisure, culture, and love of home and home-life increase among us. This improvement will go on; the modifications which our climates and modes of life suggest in existing styles will assume definite, and artistic, and permanent shape, and the new American style or styles will receive their birth. In the mean time, we must borrow and modify as best we may.

The various modes of building now in use, so far as they are susceptible of classification, may be referred to two original styles of which they are modifications—the Grecian, in which horizontal lines prevail, and the Gothic, in which vertical lines prevail. To the former class belongs the Italian, the Swiss, the Flemish, and other continental European modes, in their various modifications; and to the latter the old English styles of various periods, as well as the modern rural Gothic mode.

In adopting any mode for imitation, our preference should be guided not only by the intrinsic beauty which we see in a particular style, but by its appropriateness to our uses. This will generally be indicated by the climate, the site, and the wants of the family which is to inhabit the house. In high northern latitudes, where colonnades and verandas would be unsuitable, the Grecian or Italian styles should not be chosen; and in a tropical one, the warm, solid, comfortable features of the old English architecture would be neither necessary nor appropriate.*

1. Taking the climate alone into consideration, a Southern should differ in many respects from a Northern house. The broad halls, airy rooms, cool ombras, and spacious verandas or arcades and balconies, required by the former, seem to indicate a modification of the Italian style; while the compact arrangement of apartments, the provisions for fireside comfort, and the protection against heavy snows which must be insisted upon in the latter, point to the various forms of the Gothic rural style. In the middle region of our country, either style may appropriately be adopted, as other conditions may require.

2. The next consideration is fitness to the site we have chosen, or harmony with the scenery around. "Rural architecture," it has been truly said, "is the creation of a picture

* Downing.

of which the landscape is the background." We must design the principal object in the picture to correspond with its accessories. "The ultimate test of rural architecture and its kindred art, landscape gardening, is landscape painting. Does a literal view of a building and its environs from a well-chosen point, or from several points of view, make a good picture? Does it, as artists say, *compose* well? Does it seem of a piece, as if the building might have grown out of the ground? Then, but not otherwise, the design is good."*

The principle here laid down is violated by erecting a Swiss *chalêt* in a low, flat country; a small, plain, unpretending cottage on an elevated and commanding situation; or an Italian villa with a lookout tower in a secluded valley. It should also be understood that rustic features look well only in the midst of rural simplicity, and that architectural elegance should be reserved for cultivated scenes. Again, where the features of the landscape are wild and grand, irregularity and picturesqueness in the forms of buildings may appropriately be introduced. A cottage which would seem fitting and beautiful on a village street would be incongruous with its situation and appear evidently misplaced on a rough hillside, in the midst of the wildness of nature.

3. The plan of a house, as we have already said, should be made with reference to its site. The style and character of the elevation are influenced in some measure by the plan. Some plans, however, are adapted to various styles of elevation, while others are well suited to only one. The size determined upon will also modify the character of a house, and must always be taken into the account.

4. The materials to be used in construction will also necessarily influence one in the choice of a style; for although a given design may perhaps be executed in either wood, brick, or stone, it will not be equally adapted to each. Variety of form and profusion of ornament are attained in stone and brick only

---

* Gervase Wheeler.

at great expense. Rural cottages of these materials should therefore generally be simple in form, and depend for their effect upon proportion, symmetry, and what artists call *breadth*, rather than upon variety and picturesqueness of outline and high finish. In wood, greater variety of form and more elaborate embellishment may be secured at a given expense; indeed, so great is the facility of producing architectural ornaments in this material, that they are too often applied unmeaningly, uselessly, and to a most absurd extent.

5. One hint more on this head for the especial benefit of those who have spent most of their lives in cities. Do not carry your cockneyism into the country. Leave your town house where it is. It is, no doubt, a very good town house; but nothing can be more absurd than to attempt to reproduce it in the midst of orchards and cornfields. Downing speaks of a suburban villa which he saw on Long Island in the shape of "a narrow, unmistakable 'six story brick,' which seemed in its forlornness and utter want of harmony with all about it, as if it had strayed out of town in a fit of insanity and had lost the power of getting back again." "A word to the wise," etc.

V.—MATERIALS.

1. *Wood.*—No other material is so extensively employed in rural architecture, in this country, as wood. This arises mainly from its abundance and cheapness; but an additional reason for its use may be found in its *suitableness* for the kind of buildings mostly wanted, and its truthful expression of the unstable and migratory character of our people. Temporary shelters, rather than permanent homes, have been in demand. Young men expecting soon to be able to build villas or mansions, have not cared to erect cottages of stone or brick, to be pulled down or sold in the course of a few years. Wood is just the thing required. And when the time arrives for building the villa or the mansion (for these castles in the air, in many cases, ultimately assume a tangible shape on the solid ground), the projector is perhaps no longer young

Wood will still serve his purpose. Why should he seek a more enduring material? He will need the building but a few years; and his sons, perhaps, have all "gone West"—at any rate, they will sell the paternal mansion so soon as it shall come into their possession and build for themselves. It has for them none of the sacred associations of home. It is haunted by no memories of their childhood. It is only their father's grand new house!

So it has been in the past, and so, to a large extent, will it continue to be for a long time to come; but there is a tendency, as we have before hinted, toward a better state of things. In the older parts of the country, at least, families are acquiring local permanency, and a love of home and all that pertains to home-life and home-scenes is beginning to be fostered. These circumstances and sentiments will gradually find expression in a more solid and enduring style of domestic architecture.

But while wood is abundant and comparatively cheap, it will necessarily continue to be employed by those who must build cheaply or not at all. Rent-paying is distasteful to our people, who choose rather to live in houses of low cost owned by themselves, than to go and come at the beck of a landlord. They are right; and while we would gladly see them give place to better and more permanent ones, we are proud of the flimsy, unsubstantial structures, so sneered at by foreigners, which dot the whole face of the country. They are the homes of the people, who will by-and-by build and own better ones.

For all wooden cottages, Downing recommends vertical boarding with inch or inch and a quarter pine, tongued and grooved at the edges, nailed on, and covered with neat battens. We think, however, that filled-in walls are to be preferred. These are made by filling-in a course of any cheap bricks from bottom to top of the whole frame. This will make a wall four inches thick between the weather-boarding and the lath and plastering of the rooms. The cheapest mortar, made with a small proportion of lime, is used for this filling-in; some place the bricks on edge and build them flush with the inside of the timbers or studs (or, rather, projecting a quarter of an inch forward). This leaves a hollow space between the weather-boarding and the brick wall, and renders lathing unnecessary, the plaster being applied directly on the inner face of the filling-in.

2. *Stone.*—Where permanence is required, and the style of architecture adopted will admit it, stone is undoubtedly the best of all materials for building. In some parts of the country, however, it can not be procured; and even when it is abundant, the expense of quarrying, shaping, and laying it up, generally renders the first cost of a stone house much greater than that of a wooden one. But where the cost of preparing the stone is small, it may often be advantageously used in building houses of moderate cost.

The inner face of the walls of stone houses should always be "furred off," leaving a space of two or more inches between the solid wall and the plaster. The stratum of air thus interposed will effectually prevent dampness, and render the wall cooler in summer and warmer in winter than it could otherwise be made.*

In damp situations it is also necessary to build the foundation walls of hydraulic lime mortar, to cut off the access of moisture from the ground. With those precautions, houses built of stone will be as free from dampness as any other.

3. *Brick.*—Brick, when made of good clay, rightly tempered with sand, and well burned, makes an excellent material for building, either in city, village, or country. It is suitable for designs in which stone can not, without great expense, be wrought into the required forms.

Hollow walls are best for brick houses, their advantages being: 1. A considerable saving of materials; 2. The prevention of dampness; 3. The saving of all the cost of lathing and studding for the interior walls; 4. The great security afforded

* For an excellent method of building with unhewn stone, see Appendix (A).

against fire; 5. The opportunity they afford for thorough and easily controlled ventilation.* When not built hollow, brick walls should be "furred off" in the same way as those of stone.

When timber and stone are both scarce, as on the prairies of the West, cottages and farm-houses are frequently built of unburnt brick. In our Appendix will be found an account of their construction, condensed from a Report on the subject made by Mr. Ellsworth while Commissioner of Patents. He bears the strongest testimony to their cheapness, warmth, and durability.†

4. *Concrete.*—Much attention has been directed of late to walls of concrete for country houses. These walls are said to combine in a high degree durability, cheapness, warmth, and dryness. They are composed of lime, sand, gravel, and fragments of stone. A considerable number of houses have been built of this material within the last few years, with varying and seemingly contradictory results. In some cases perfect success seems to have been attained, the walls assuming and retaining a stone-like consistency and promising great durability, while in others expensive failures have been the result, the structures crumbling to powder within two years.

Our own opinion, formed after a thorough examination of the subject, is, that where all the requisite materials abound, walls of concrete may be put up far more cheaply than those of stone or brick, and that a durability nearly equal to that of marble may be universally secured by a strict compliance with the following conditions:

1. The various materials entering into the composition of the concrete must be well selected and rightly compounded—the lime being of a good quality, the sand clean and sharp, and the gravel well screened, and each of these ingredients, as well as the rock fragments, being used in the proper proportion.

2. The walls must be built at the proper season of the year, to insure their perfect hardening before being affected by frost.

---

* See Appendix (B).

† See Appendix (C).

3. The building must be covered by a projecting roof, to protect the walls against vertical rains.

We have yet to learn that a failure has ever occurred where all these conditions have been strictly adhered to.

We give in the Appendix some account of the mode of building concrete walls, and further information may be found in O. S. Fowler's "Home for All."* Our principal objection to this mode of building lies in the necessity which exists for external plastering or stuccoing, and the consequent blank and monotonous appearance of the walls. With many persons, however, this objection will have little weight. It may be obviated by the common sham of marking off the surface in imitation of courses of stone, an untruthful practice which we can not recommend.

VI.—MISCELLANEOUS DETAILS.

1. *Cellars.*—Cellars under dwelling houses are generally deemed indispensable. They are certainly very useful; but there is an evil of such magnitude connected with them, that some have advocated their entire abolition. They are almost universally manufactories and reservoirs of foul air, which, finding its way upward by means of doors, windows, stairways, and crevices in the floors, diffuses its noxious elements through the rooms above, and becomes a fruitful source of disease. It is not necessary that they should be half filled with rotting garbage to produce this result. The surface of the earth is filled with decomposable substances, and whenever air is confined in any spot in contact with the ground, or any changeable organic matter, it becomes saturated with various exhalations which are detrimental to health.† Means must be provided, therefore, for their thorough ventilation, or cellars must be abandoned altogether.‡

A cellar, to fully serve its purposes, should be cool in sum-

---

* Published by Fowler and Wells; price, 87 cents. † Professor Youmans.
‡ See Appendix (D).

mer, impervious to frost in winter, and dry at all times. The walls should rise one or two feet at least above the level of the surrounding ground, and should be laid in good lime mortar, or at least pointed with it. The thickness of the wall should not be less than from fifteen to eighteen inches; and if the house walls above be built of brick or stone, two feet is better. The cellar should have a drain from the lowest corner, which should be always kept open; and each room in it should have at least two sliding sash windows, to secure a circulation of air. In very cold climates, those portions of the walls above the surface of the ground should be double, either by means of a distinct thin wall on the outside or by lathing and plastering on the inside, and be furnished with double windows as a further security against frost. An outside door with a flight of steps is desirable in every cellar, and in one connected with a farm-house indispensable.

2. *Chimneys.*—The construction of an effective chimney would seem to be a very simple and easy matter; and so it is, provided the philosophical principles involved be first understood, as they should be by every builder.

Fig. 2.

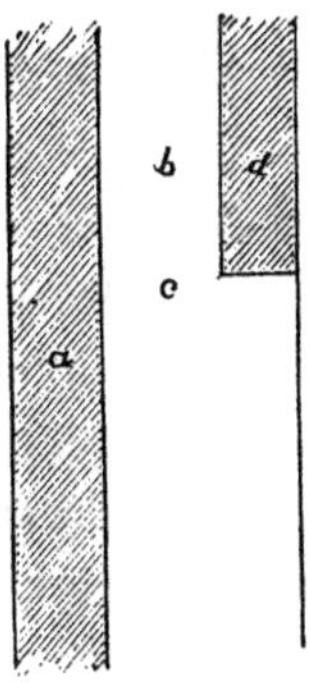

FAULTY CONSTRUCTION.

Fig. 3.

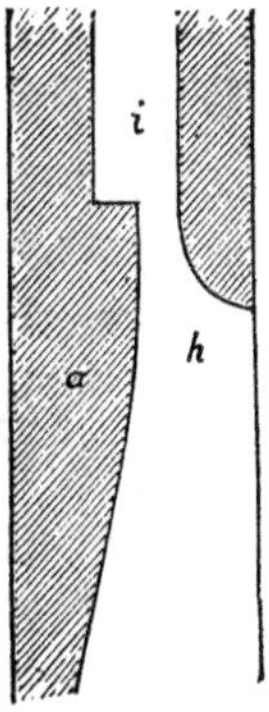

CORRECT CONSTRUCTION.

The main point to be attended to in order to cause a chimney to draw well, is to contract the openings both at the throat and at the top, so as to break the force of any downward currents of air which may be thrown into it. Fig. 2 will serve to illustrate the faulty construction of the throat, and fig. 3 the correct construction.

In very windy or exposed situations the top of the chimney should be contracted to a third less than the area of the flue; but in ordinary cases a diminution of about two inches in the diameter will be sufficient.

3. *Warming.*—The original plan for warming houses was to build a fire in the center of the principal room, the smoke being allowed to find its way out either at a hole in the roof or through any accidental crevices which might exist. With the invention of the chimney came the fire-place, an opening in the side of its base. This opening formed, at first, an immense recess with square side-walls or jambs, and, in addition to the fire, furnished accommodations for several persons, who were provided with seats within its area. The tendency of modern improvement has been to gradually contract this opening, until it seems in a fair way to be abolished altogether; but this last step should not be taken till something more suitable than has yet been produced shall have been provided to take its place.

The principal methods of warming now in use in this country are: 1. By open fire-places; 2. By open grates; 3. By stoves; 4. By hot-air furnaces; 5. By steam and hot-water apparatuses.

1. The open fire-place furnishes the pleasantest and most healthful mode of warming a room; but in a pecuniary point of view it is not economical. A very large portion of the heat generated is carried up the chimney and lost. By so constructing the fire-place that it may supply a current of heated air to the room, which may easily be done in various ways, this objection is partially obviated.

Any attempt to bring the fire-place again into general use, even in the country, would probably be vain; but we can not refrain from expressing most emphatically our opinion, that in places where fuel is still cheap, the substitution of stoves has been a most unwise and short-sighted piece of false economy. Shall we give up the cheerful and healthful glow of the blazing fire, and submit to the stifling heat and gloomy appearance of the deadly "air-tight," for the mere purpose of saving a few dollars, at the expense of an untold amount of health and comfort? We must at least put on record here our earnest protest against it.

2. Next to the open fire-place, in point of health and comfort, comes the open chimney grate. Similar to this, and more economical, is the stove grate or open stove. This, when properly constructed with an air-chamber within it connected with the open air by a pipe and with several openings near the top to admit the warmed air into the room, furnishes a very pleasant means of warming an apartment.

3. Our opinion of stoves has already been hinted at. If it conflicts with the generally received ideas on the subject, we can not help it. With the exception of the open stove or stove grate already mentioned, we are constrained to pronounce them unmitigated nuisances, entirely unworthy of acceptance in an enlightened age and by an enlightened people. They have not a single advantage, so far as we can perceive, to recommend them—not even that of economy, for where they subtract one dollar from the fuel account, they add two to the doctor's bill.

We believe that their almost universal introduction has had more to do than any other single cause with the acknowledged deterioration which has taken place within the last half century in the health and vital stamina of our people. It is Dickens, we believe, who calls the stove the "household demon." Would to God we had the power to exorcise it!

4. Hot-air furnaces, steam apparatus, etc., are little used in warming small country houses; and it is hardly desirable that they should be more extensively introduced; for their advantages, as they are generally managed, are fully counterbalanced by their disadvantages.

In building, attention should be directed to making the walls of a dwelling-house poor conductors of heat. Of the means of doing this we have already spoken. For the same reason double windows should be introduced wherever the winters are very severe. Ordinary windows, no matter how tight they may be, are great abstractors of heat—or, rather, they furnish a medium through which the cold air without abstracts the heat from the warm air within. Double windows, by con fining a stratum of air (a non-conductor of heat) between them, entirely prevents this loss. Doubling the glass in the same sash answers the purpose equally well.

5. *Ventilation.*—We can not here go into an exposition of the relations of atmospheric air to the animal economy, or show how its various constituents affect the system. We must take it for granted that the reader understands and fully appreciates the fact, that pure air is quite as essential to the health of the body and the right performance of its functions as wholesome food, and that therefore a copious and constant supply of it in our dwellings is of the utmost importance. But this, we fear, is assuming too much. If it be generally known that the atmospheric air in its purity, and that alone, is fitted for the respiration of human beings, how does it happen that the great mass of our people are content to breathe, during a large portion of their lives, a vile compound of noxious gases instead? In a majority of our houses, even of the better sort, the little ventilation which takes place is purely incidental, no direct provision whatever being made for it. What is the result? During the warmest weather of summer, open doors and windows generally secure adequate circulation and consequent purity of air. In the winter, and a portion of the time in the summer, the case is quite different. The windows and doors are carefully closed and a fire kindled in the stove or grate, around which we gather. Now commences the transformation of the life-giving element, with which the room was originally filled, into a subtile but active and powerful agent of disease and death. The air, chemists tell us, is mainly composed of nitrogen and oxygen, of which the latter is the active, life-giving principle, and the former the neutral or diluting principle. Now each person takes into his lungs more than two hogsheads per hour of this vital fluid—that is, provided it can be had—retains most of the oxygen, and throws out in place of it nearly an equal bulk of carbonic acid gas—a deadly poison. The combustion of fuel in the stove or grate, and of the substances

used in lighting the room in the evening, acts upon the air in nearly the same manner as breathing—consuming its oxygen and supplying its place with carbonic acid. Other gaseous impurities, among which is carbonic oxyd, a much more deadly poison than carbonic acid even, are thrown out by our stoves, and particularly by those called "air tight," to add to the general mass of impurity which we compel ourselves to breathe. What must soon become the state of the atmosphere in a closed room under these circumstances? Does it startle you to think of it? Well it may! Depend upon it, if you could *see* the mass of vitiated and poisoned air in the midst of which you are living—if it should for a moment become visible in the form of a sickly, yellow mist or a cloud of lurid, deadly red, and you were really aware of all its noxious properties—you would flee from your stove-heated and unventilated rooms as from a city swept by a pestilence. What wonder we have headaches and bad digestion; that the cheek of beauty grows pale among us and the eye of youth dim and sunken; that the vital powers are gradually undermined; and that scrofula, dyspepsia, and consumption are so common and so fatal. But have we not said enough? There is a remedy—

☞ VENTILATION, ☜

and if you forget everything else in this little book—if you heed our advice on no other point—remember this injunction: *Never build a house, or live in one already built, without providing adequate means for the thorough ventilation of every room in it.*

Ventilation embraces two distinct processes—the removal of the foul air and the introduction of pure air; and to be satisfactory, both must be carried on without producing injurious or offensive currents.

The simplest provision for the escape of bad air is an opening in the chimney near the ceiling, properly provided with a valve or register. This mode of ventilation is simple, easily introduced even into houses already built, and thoroughly effective, at least while fires are kept up, as they usually are during the winter, when ventilation is most required. An Arnot valve is better than a register for insertion in a chimney opening, since it effectually prevents the escape of smoke into the room. This valve is a very simple box of cast iron, with an iron valve so contrived that it will remain open while there is the least pressure of foul air from within, but close at once against any current in the opposite direction. It is easily built into the chimney, or can be inserted afterward by merely taking out two or three bricks.

Fig. 4.

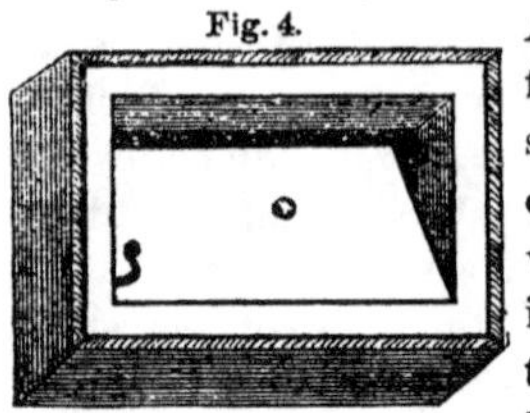

ARNOT'S VALVE.

But carbonic acid gas is heavier than common air, and although carried upward by the ascending currents and partially drawn off by the opening near the ceiling, a portion of it descends and forms a stratum in the lower part of the room. The current kept up by the combustion going on in an open fire-place or a grate helps to draw this off; but it is essential to perfect ventilation that an opening near the floor be provided for the special purpose of carrying it away. A square piece of wire gauze inserted in the lower part of the fire-board, with a curtain of oiled silk behind it, to serve as a valve, will answer this purpose tolerably well, where the chimney current is sufficiently strong. Apertures connected with downward conducting flues, however, are generally more serviceable.

Means being provided for the escape of the impure air, a partial supply of fresh air from outside finds its way into our rooms through accidental fissures and occasionally opened doors; but it is irregular and inadequate. More may be intro duced by lowering the upper sash of a window, but this creates an unpleasant and dangerous current of cold air, and is therefore unsatisfactory. An improvement upon this plan is to replace one of the upper panes of glass in the window farthest from the fire by a perforated plate of zinc or a *louvre* made of tin, zinc, or glass, with horizontal openings or slats like a

Venetian blind. A contrivance of this nature is far better than no provision at all for the admission of pure air, and should always be resorted to when no better arrangement may be practicable. But the best way to introduce fresh air is through air-chambers connected with the fire-place or grate, so that it may be warmed before being thrown into the room. An arrangement of this kind, connected with an open fire-place or grate, is represented by figs. 5 and 6. The fresh air enters from the outside at *a*. Fig. 5 is slightly warmed in the air-chamber at the back or side of the fire-place, *b*, and passes into the room by a side opening, as shown at *a*, fig. 6. The valve for the escape of the bad air is represented by *b*, fig. 6. It is better, however, that the opening for the admission of fresh air and the valve for the escape of impure air should be on opposite sides of the chimney-breast.*

Fig. 5.

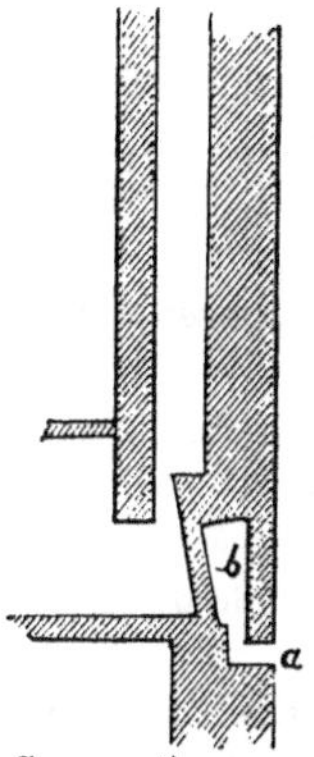

CHIMNEY SECTION.

Fig. 6.

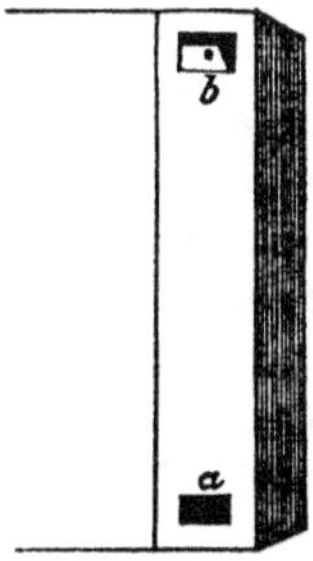

CHIMNEY OPENINGS.

But a perfect system of ventilation, effective at all seasons and operating in all the apartments of the house, whether furnished with fire-places or not, requires a series of ventilating flues (the openings in which must be provided with the necessary valves), all leading into a larger flue or shaft in which a current is constantly kept up, both winter and summer. The kitchen fire furnishes the motive power required. It may be effectively applied in various ways as circumstances may require and ingenuity suggest, aided, if necessary, by a ventilating cap at the top of the shaft. Having mastered the principles on which ventilation depends, as every one purposing to build a house should do, the rest will be easy.

---

* Downing.

In providing for the ventilation of your house, give special attention to the *nursery* and the *sleeping-rooms*, and do not forget the *cellar*. The last, if provided with the outside door and sliding sash windows we have recommended, may be tolerably well ventilated in summer, while these can be left open, without extra provision for that purpose; but in the winter the operation of a ventilating flue extended down from an active chimney flue is absolutely essential to anything like purity of air in such an underground apartment.

6. *Exterior Color.*—For the outside painting of country houses, quiet, neutral tints should generally be chosen. The various shades of fawn, drab, gray, and brown, are all very suitable. All the positive colors, such as red, yellow, blue, green, black, and white, should always be avoided. Nothing can be in worse taste than the very common practice of painting country houses white. This color is glaring and disagreeable to the eye, when presented in large masses; it makes a house an obtrusive and too conspicuous object in the landscape; it does not harmonize with the hues of nature—standing, as it were, harshly apart from all the soft shades of the scene. *Use any other color rather than white.* Downing makes an exception to this rule in favor of cottages deeply embowered in trees—the shadow of the foliage taking away the harshness and offensiveness of the color; but even in such cases we would modify the white by a slight admixture of chrome yellow and Indian red. Red, another glaring and disagreeable color, is a common one for farm-houses in some parts of the country. It is scarcely less offensive to the eye than white.

Perceiving the absurdity of painting country houses white, many have gone to the other extreme, and given their dwellings a too dark and somber hue. Light, cheerful, but unobtrusive colors, harmonizing with the prevailing hues of the country, are most suitable. Take the colors of the various earths, the stones, the trunks and branches of trees, mosses, and other natural objects for your guides, and you will not go far wrong. A quiet fawn color or drab and a warm gray—that is, a gray mixed with a very little red and some yellow—are the safest colors to recommend for general use. The browns and dark grays are suitable for stables and out-buildings.

A mansion or a villa should have a somewhat sober hue; a house of moderate size a light and pleasant tone; and a small cottage a still lighter and livelier tint. A house exposed to the view should have a darker hue than one that is much hidden by foliage.

To produce the best effect, several tints or shades of color should be used in painting the exterior of a house; and it is important that they be judiciously chosen and combined. If the color selected for the main walls be *light*, the facings of the windows, the roof trimmings, verandas, etc., may appropriately be a darker shade of the same color; and if the prevailing color of the building be *dark*, a lighter shade should be applied to the trimmings. If Venetian blinds be used, the solid parts of them may be similar in shade to the window casings, but a little darker, and the movable slats darkest of all. If green be preferred for the blinds, it should be a very dark green; light and bright greens having a flashy and disagreeable effect.

6. *Interior Color*, *Wall Paper*, *etc.*—Instead of painting and graining interior wood-work in imitation of oak, black walnut, or other dark wood, Downing recommends to stain it, so as to give the effect of the darker wood while retaining the real appearance of the grain of the pine or other wood itself. We give in the Appendix his recipe for staining pine and other soft woods.

The remarks made in the preceding section in reference to colors will apply with slight modification to the interiors as well as the exteriors of houses. Agreeable neutral tints—gray, drab, fawn color, etc.—should be given to the walls, the ceilings alone being white, the cost of a wash of these tints for a room being only a few cents greater than that of a whitewash. When walls are to be papered, colors and patterns should be chosen with reference to the same principles. If architectural paper be used, it must be in the same style as the house—an Italian or Grecian room in a Gothic cottage not being quite appropriate.

The best effect is produced by having the ceiling lightest, the side walls a little darker, the wood-work a shade darker still, and the carpet darkest of all.* The hall and all passages and staircases should be of a cool, sober tone of color, and simple in decoration.

7. *Roofing.*—For the general purposes of roofing for country houses there is no good material perhaps so generally available as shingles. Slate forms an excellent covering, but in most localities is far too costly for ordinary use. Tin serves a good purpose when well put on; but on account of its tendency to expand and contract, is somewhat liable to get out of order. Thick canvas is good for the flat roofs of verandas and other small surfaces.†

8. *Stucco.*—Stuccoing or outside plastering has been tried to a considerable extent in this country; but generally with indifferent success. The stucco, so far as our observation extends, soon cracks and begins to peel off under the sudden and fierce alternations of heat and cold to which our climate is subject. Mr. Downing—high authority in such matters—however, speaks favorably of stuccoing for rough walls, and expresses the opinion that the cause of its failure is that it is so imperfectly understood, and consequently so badly practiced in this country. We copy his directions in our Appendix.‡

9. *Rough-Cast.*—Rough-cast is a species of cheap and durable cement adapted to farm-houses and the plainer kind of rural cottages. It is adapted, like stucco, to rough walls. See Appendix for directions for preparing and applying it.§

10. *Drainage.*—Efficient drainage for the sewerage and waste water must be provided for in every plan for a country house. Four or five inch earthen pipes are best to connect

* Downing.

† See Appendix (F) for something more about roofing materials.

‡ (F.) § Ibid.

the cess-pool with the house. They must be "trapped," so that there shall be no continuous air-passage through which noxious gases may rise. The cess-pool must not be near the well.

11. *Trees, Shrubs, and Vines.*—We have no space to devote to landscape gardening, which, although closely related to rural architecture, lies beyond the scope of our plan. We can only say, plant trees, shrubs, and vines by all means; but call taste and judgment to your aid in choosing and arranging them. The largest masses of foliage should not be placed in front, but should flank and form a background for the house. Placed too near a house, trees of dense foliage create dampness, injure the walls and roof, and impede the circulation of the air. A drapery of vines creeping or trailing over them, and twining around the porches, verandas, and windows, are among the most beautiful and appropriate decorations for a cottage; and they are within the reach of everybody and should be universally employed. See "The Garden"* for lists of ornamental trees, shrubs, and vines, and directions for planting them.

VII.—COMMON ERRORS AND ABSURDITIES.

The errors and absurdities in rural architecture committed in this country (and other countries are not free from them) are too numerous to admit even an enumeration here. The following are a few of the commonest and most glaring ones:

1. Building a cottage of the dimensions of twenty feet by thirty, in imitation of a Grecian temple, with lofty columns of painted wood, forming a grand portico in front.

2. Building castellated villas with towers and battlements of thin pine boards.

3. Illustrating the Gothic style "run mad," in wooden cottages composed principally of gables, and looking, Downing says, as if they had been "knocked into a cocked hat."

4. Giving examples of all the principal styles of architecture

* The Garden: a Pocket Manual of Practical Horticulture—the second number of the series. [Price, in paper, 30 cents; in muslin, 50 cents.]

in the same house—the roof, for instance, belonging to one style and age; the doors and windows to another; and the porches and verandas to a third. Corinthian columns supporting Gothic arches! Very fine!

5. Imitating a villa in a diminutive cottage, and covering it all over with frippery and "gingerbread work."

6. Supposing that ornament and beauty in architecture are synonymous, and consist in something extraneous and superadded.

7. Building houses to look at rather than to live in, and thereby making them "distressingly fine."

8. Finishing and furnishing a splendid parlor for visitors and to "show off," and living in a bare-walled, smoky, uncomfortable kitchen all one's life.

9. Imitating marble and granite in lath and plaster, and oak and walnut in soft pine and hemlock.

10. Surrounding a house in the extreme North with verandas or arcades, and building a Southern one without them.

11. Mounting outside Venetian blinds upon a Gothic cottage or villa.

12. Building a Swiss *chalêt* or cottage on a level village street, or a narrow, three-story brick house to stand dignifiedly apart in a wild, secluded valley.

13. Painting country houses white or red.

14. Building in haste to repent at leisure; or building a house first and planning it afterward.

15. Building temporary *shelters* instead of *homes.*

III.

COTTAGES OF ONE STORY.

I knew by the smoke that so gracefully curled
Above the green elms, that a cottage was near.—*Moore.*

I.—PRELIMINARY REMARKS.

A COTTAGE of one story, in the sense in which we shall employ the term, is one in which the side walls do not rise above the second floor, which forms, as it were, the base of the roof.

When properly constructed, such cottages are both convenient and attractive. They favor economy of labor (no climbing of stairs being required), and are pleasing and unobtrusive objects in the landscape; while small houses, carried up two or three stories in height, although they may be economically built, are far less conducive to labor saving, and, in the country at least, present a most unsightly appearance.

The foundation walls of all low cottages should be raised somewhat above the level of the surrounding ground. They should be plain and simple in style and finish, the foliage of creeping and climbing plants furnishing their most appropriate ornament.

In the designs which follow, we have endeavored to keep in mind the wants of small families of limited means, and have aimed to show how the largest amount of convenience and comfort may be secured for the smallest sum of money, and at the same time to impress upon the reader's mind the fact that, because a cottage may be small and cheap, it need not therefore the ugly. Taste need not always necessarily add to expense, and the expression of beauty need not be lacking even in the rudest cabin or shanty.

II.—A LOG CABIN.

As our first design, we present a log cabin—a kind of dwelling which must continue to be common for a long time to come, in

Fig. 7.

PERSPECTIVE VIEW.

parts of the West and South. The plan requires no explanation. Space may be saved by building an outside chimney at each end, instead of the central one represented in the plan. In a warm climate the former is the better mode; but the unsightly projections thus formed should be covered with climbing and creeping plants. Nowhere can the Virginia creeper, the ivy, the jasmine, the trumpet flower, the clematis, the climbing roses, etc., be more appropriately disposed than around the veranda, windows, and gables of a log cabin. Our artist has been rather sparing of them, as also of trees in the accompanying design, but they should be supplied in abundance. They are cheap adornments, and come within the reach of all. In their proper place, the skill of the best architect can substitute nothing equally satisfactory.

The leading external feature in the foregoing perspective view is the veranda in front, covered by the projecting roof. Its rustic posts should be covered with vines, among which the grape might appropriately have a place.

Fig. 8.

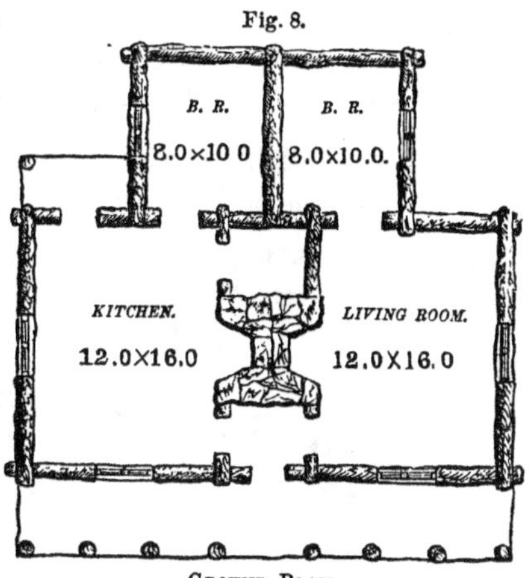

GROUND PLAN.

III.—A HEXAGON PLAN.

A Western correspondent, Mr. W. Holly, of St. Louis, furnishes the accompanying as an economical, simple, and convenient plan for inclosing and dividing a given space. The rooms, it will be seen, are all of the same size and form, and present the most compact arrangement possible. A single chimney, in the center, furnishes fire-places for them all. Omitting its fire-place, the bed-room might be divided by a partition in the center, thus giving two small sleeping apartments. With plain walls and a flat roof, such a house could be put up

Fig. 9.

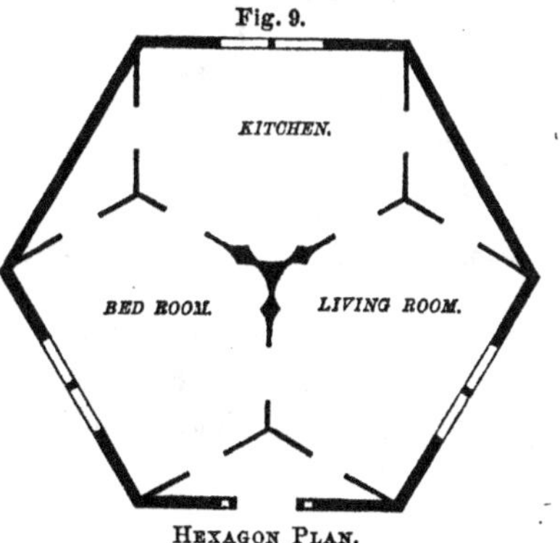

HEXAGON PLAN.

on the prairies or in the forests of the West for a very small sum; and we do not see how the same amount of accommodation can be more economically obtained.

IV.—A PLAN FOR THREE ROOMS, ETC.

This excellent plan for a three-roomed cottage is borrowed, with modifications, from "Village and Farm Cottages" by Cleveland & Backus Brothers. It explains itself; and we venture to say that a better arrangement of the same amount of space can not easily be devised. A plain but substantial and pleasing little structure on this plan, with the inside walls all neatly papered, a low projecting roof, and plain hoods over the windows, would cost, in this vicinity, from $550 to $650. The laundry and wood-room would naturally be covered by a lean-to roof, or they might be omitted. If a cellar should be required, it might be under the kitchen, and entered from the wood-room.

Fig. 10.

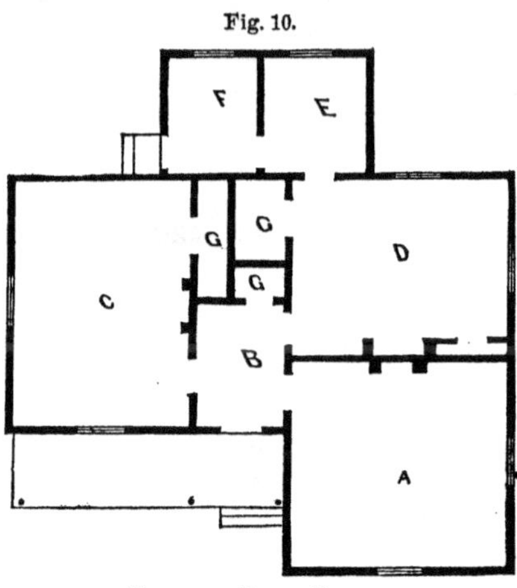

PLAN FOF THREE ROOMS.

A—Living Room	14.0 × 15.0
B—Hall	6.0 × 8.0
C—Bed Room	12 0 × 16.6
D—Kitchen	12 0 × 15.0
E—Wood Room	7.0 × 8.0
F—Laundry	6.0 × 8.0
G—Closets	

ESTIMATES.—The circumstances on which the cost of a house will depend vary so greatly with time and place, that estimates made without a knowledge of these circumstances are only useful as a basis of comparison and calculation. Where estimates are given in this work, they are calculated for the vicinity of New York, and based on the following valuation:

Timber	at $20 00	per	1,000	feet.
Rough boards	" 20 00	"	"	"
Good lumber (planed)	" 22 00	"	"	"
Bricks	" 6 00	"	"	
Nails	" 05	"	lb.	
Glass	" 4 00	"	box.	
Carpenter's work	" 1 75	"	day.	
Mason's work	" 1 75	"	"	
Common labor	" 1 00	"	"	

Whenever the cost of labor and materials is greater or less than that given in the foregoing table, the proper allowance must be made.

V.—A SOUTHERN COTTAGE.

This differs widely from all our previous designs, and indicates its adaptation to a different climate and different social

Fig. 11.

PERSPECTIVE VIEW.

customs and habits. Its principal features are the veranda, which extends on all sides, and the broad hall running through the center. This hall furnishes access to every room, and facilitates a free circulation of air through the house. The living-room and the large bed-room may change places, where the situation and aspect render such a change desirable. The bay

Fig. 12.

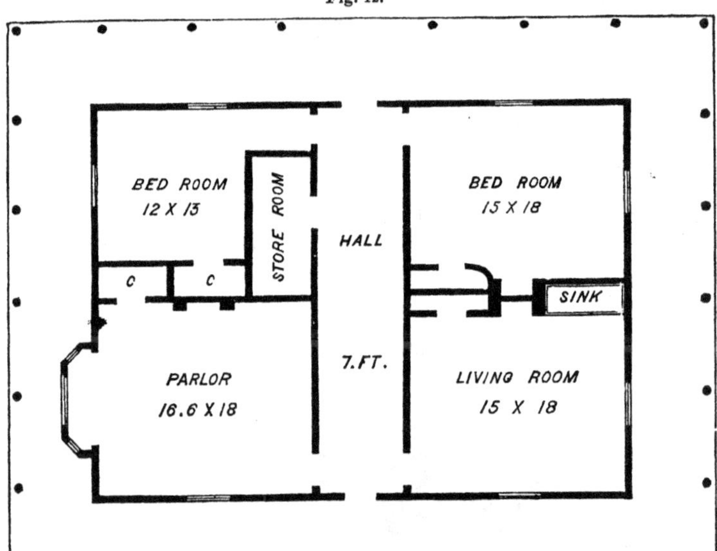

PLAN OF A SOUTHERN COTTAGE.

window adds much to the beauty and comfort of the parlor, but may be omitted if considerations of economy require.

The elevation is plain but not unattractive, and, in its external features, very distinctly expresses its character as a Southern dwelling.

This will be found a comfortable and convenient home for a planter of small estate and means, or for an overseer on a large plantation. Its cost will vary much in different parts of the South. Built of wood, as represented in our perspective view, from $650 to $700 would perhaps be an average estimate.

VERANDAS.*—The veranda is an essential feature of the Southern house. It should extend the entire length of two sides, at least, and it is better that it should encircle the whole building. It may, however, if desired, be either wholly or partially inclosed on the north side, forming small rooms under its roof, as shown in fig. 52. There should be ventilating hooded apertures in the roof of the veranda for the escape of the heated air, which otherwise accumulates under it.

VI.—ANOTHER CHEAP COTTAGE PLAN.

Figs. 13 and 14 represent a plan for a house which would

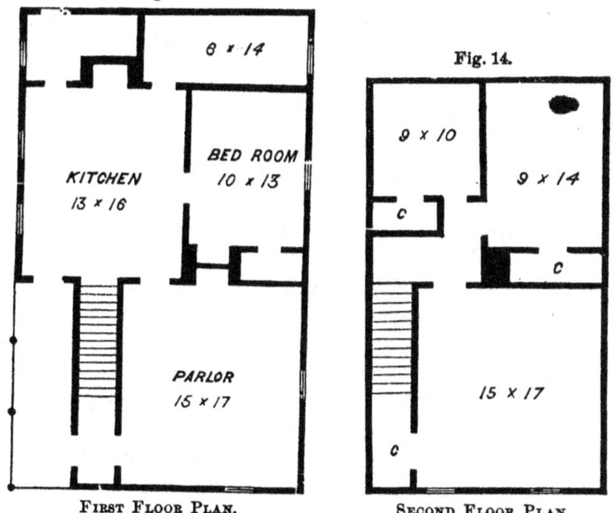

FIRST FLOOR PLAN. SECOND FLOOR PLAN.

conveniently accommodate a small family, and could be built at a small cost—say from $500 to $600. The general arrangement of the first floor is readily seen, and requires no explanation.

---

* In this country a veranda is often improperly called a *piazza*. The latter is properly a more solid structure, and is defined as "a continued archway or vaulting supported by pillars."

The veranda and projecting portion of the kitchen are to be covered by a continuation of the main roof on that side; and the store-room and large pantry back of the kitchen and bed-room by a lean-to roof. The spring of the roof above the upper floor must be high enough to give head room at the landing of the stairs. This will allow the attic to be divided, as shown by fig. 14.

DOORS.—Entrance doors should furnish means of ventilation without being opened, either by means of side-lights, or fan-lights hung on hinges, or by ornamental iron gratings with solid or glazed panels, similarly hung, on the inside.

Every entrance from without should open into a hall, entry, or lobby, to prevent the direct entrance of cold, and secure privacy.

VII.—A PLAN FOR REPEATED ADDITIONS.

It often happens that a man who may reasonably expect to be able, in the course of a few years, to build a large and handsome house, is obliged to commence with a very limited amount of means. He might procure the necessary funds, perhaps, by means of "bond and mortgage," but he chooses to take what seems to him a safer and better course. He resolves to put up so much of his house as he can pay for, and no more, even if it be but a single room; and to complete the projected structure by repeated additions, as his means accumulate. To do this advantageously the whole building must be planned at the commencement. The accompanying plans were suggested and designed to meet the requirements of a case like the one supposed.

Our enterprising, energetic, and independent proprietor (as we will suppose) of a village lot first throws up the four walls inclosing what is called in the plan the dining-room to the height of one story, and covers them with a roof; the whole being designed in strict accordance with the style of the building of which it is to form a part. The apartment thus formed constitutes for a brief period his parlor, dining-room, kitchen, and perhaps his bed-room. although if he adopts the high pitched roof he may have two small attic rooms above, reached by a staircase afterward to be removed. A lean-to, comprising the adjoining bed-room, may be cheaply erected, and is soon added. The

Fig. 15.

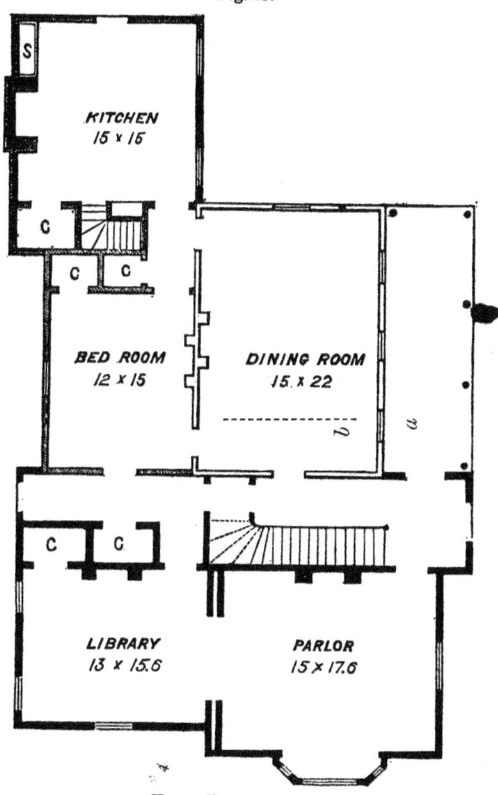

FIRST FLOOR PLAN.

kitchen, another lean-to, is next built, and the house becomes a comfortable and convenient one for a small family. Our friend can now wait several years, if necessary, before building the main edifice, represented on the plan by the black lines; interposing in the mean time, if he chooses, another story over the dining-room.

The parts now erected form quite a complete and commodious little house of themselves, and this part of the plan may be adopted, by itself, in cases in which its accommodations are

Fig. 16.

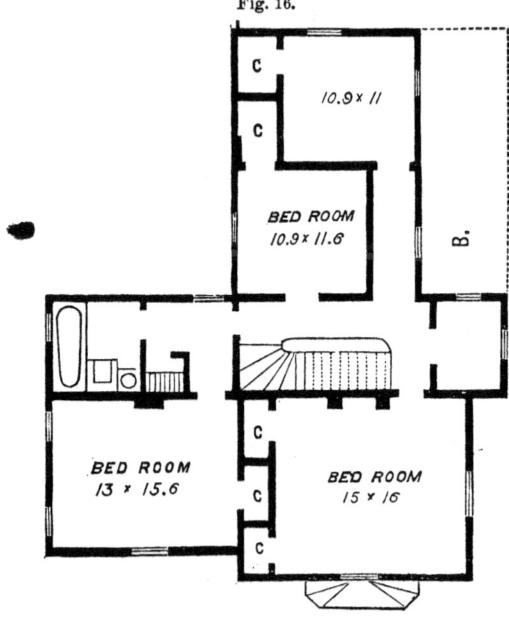

SECOND FLOOR PLAN.

sufficient. In this case, there would be a door at *a*, and a hall and staircase (for which there is ample space) at *b*, as represented by the dotted line. There is supposed to be a cellar under the dining-room and kitchen, the original part being entered at first only from the outside.

The second-floor plan shows four rooms besides a bath-room,

and ample closet accommodations. There should be a balcony at B, although not so represented in the plan.

This plan will admit a Gothic elevation, but is, perhaps, rather better adapted to the Italian style.

PLANS.—Desiring to give as large a number of plans as possible within the limits allowed us, we insert a number of them without elevations. The elevations given will illustrate the various styles of domestic architecture adapted to our climate and habits, and, with the necessary changes in general outlines, can readily be adapted to other plans.

SCALE.—Our plans, with a few exceptions specified in the proper place, are drawn to the scales of sixteen and thirty-two feet to the inch. Most of the geometrical elevations are on the scale of sixteen feet to the inch; but in the perspective views it has not been practicable to adhere to a scale.

WATER-CLOSETS.—Where running water can be introduced into a house and facilities for complete drainage exist, water-closets may be constructed in a country house without great trouble or expense, and will operate satisfactorily; but unless all the arrangements connected with them can be made perfectly *effective*, we would not advise their introduction, as they sometimes become intolerable nuisances.

As a matter of economy the bath-room and water-closets are generally placed in connection. It is decidedly preferable, however, where it is practicable to do so, to separate them entirely.

OUTSIDE PAINTING.—The best time to paint the outside of a house is late in the fall, as the paint hardens better and lasts much longer than when put on during the summer.

RATS IN CELLARS.—To prevent rats from burrowing into cellars, either make a good water-lime floor, or else build the wall on a close-jointed flagging, laid some inches below the bottom of the cellar, and projecting three or four inches beyond the wall. The rat burrows down next to the wall, reaches the flagging, and can not pass through it, never, in any case, working back to the edge.—*Rural Annual.*

VIII.—AN EXTEMPORE HOUSE.

On the prairies and in the forests of the great West the "*squatter*," or claimant of *pre-emption* right on the government lands, throws up a little cabin or shanty as one of the conditions on which he is to make his claim good. It is an *extempore* affair, but serves its purpose, and by-and-by is pulled down. It may be built of logs or of sawed lumber ; and there is no reason why it should not present as attractive and home-like an exterior as that represented below.

Fig. 17.

A WESTERN COTTAGE.

IV.

STORY-AND-A-HALF COTTAGES.

Homes for household comfort built.—*May.*

I.—PRELIMINARY REMARKS.

OUR attention will now be directed to cottages of a story and a half. In houses properly thus designated the side walls rise from two to five feet above the second floor. They usually have either dormer or low, short windows in the sides. They afford handsome and commodious chambers and are among the best and most economical of small, cheap houses, the additional expense of the half story being comparatively small.

Our designs for houses of this sort will be found, we think, to combine, so far as is possible, the qualities of economy, convenience, and beauty. They are generally compact and simple in plan, and plain but substantial in construction, and present a modest and unpretending but pleasing exterior. We have had practical utility constantly in view in designing them, and we flatter ourself that all our plans will "work"—that they will look as well and prove as satisfactory on the ground as on paper.

II.—PLANS FOR A SMALL COTTAGE.

These plans exhibit an arrangement of rooms well adapted to the use of a mechanic or laborer of small family and limited means. The living-room is a handsome apartment of good size, entered from the lobby or hall, and also communicating with the kitchen. One chimney suffices for both. The lean-to part, extended beyond the kitchen, affords space for the cellar staircase, a passage to the back entrance, a room for fuel, etc., and a large closet or pantry. The stairs by which the second floor is reached commence in the kitchen, the first two steps

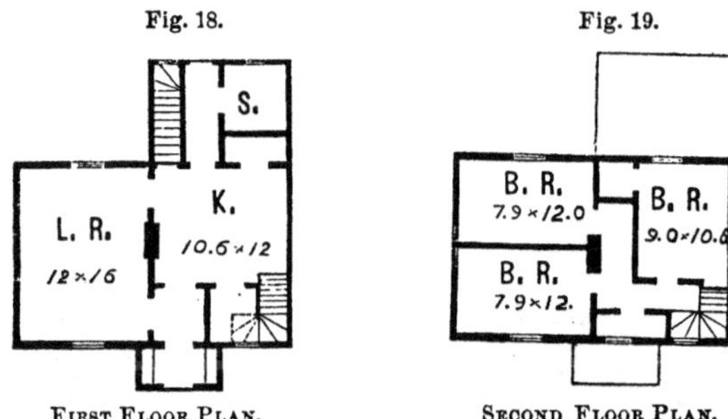

Fig. 18. FIRST FLOOR PLAN.

Fig. 19. SECOND FLOOR PLAN.

projecting beyond the wall inside. The closet next the stairs is 4.6×5 clear, besides the available space under the stairs. The chamber plan shows three sleeping apartments, with ample closet accommodations. A cellar extending under the kitchen and the lean-to part would be sufficient. This plan is on the scale of twenty-four feet to an inch. A plain and simple elevation, similar to that represented by fig. 27, would be suitable for this plan.

III.—AN ITALIAN COTTAGE.

The plans and elevations next presented were designed for this work by F. E. Graef, Architect, 56 Wall Street, New York, from whom we give several other designs, and whom we can confidently recommend to any of our patrons who may wish to obtain the services of a thoroughly educated, competent, and faithful architect.

This design is simple, and requires little explanation. A cellar under a part of the house, as shown, will be found sufficient. It is made easy of access from the kitchen, and should an outside entrance be required, it may be had at a

Fig. 20.

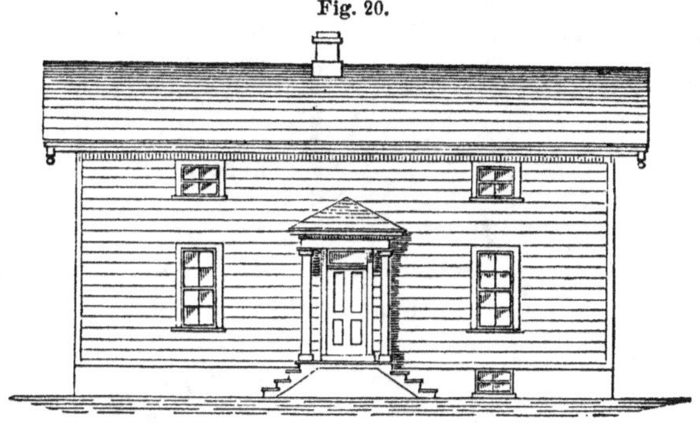

FRONT ELEVATION.

small additional expense. The first story has a main and back entrance, the former covered by a porch; a parlor; a

Fig. 21.

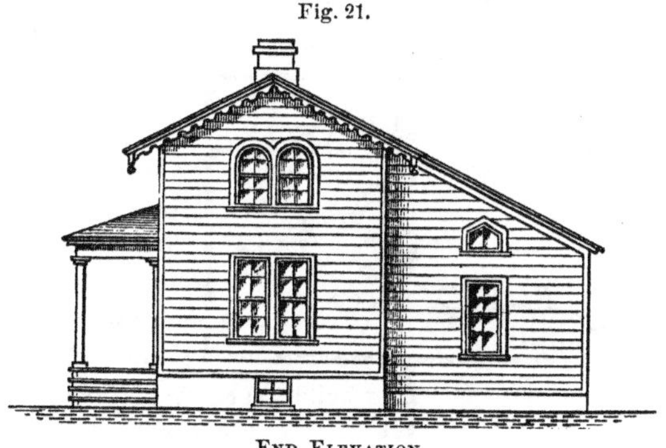

END ELEVATION.

living-room; a kitchen of good size; and ample closet accommodations.

The kitchen part of the house, in order to save expense in the foundation, and to gain more height in the garret, is set two risers, or about sixteen inches, lower than the main floor. The attic, or second floor, affords two fine bedrooms, with closets, and a useful open garret.

Fig. 22.

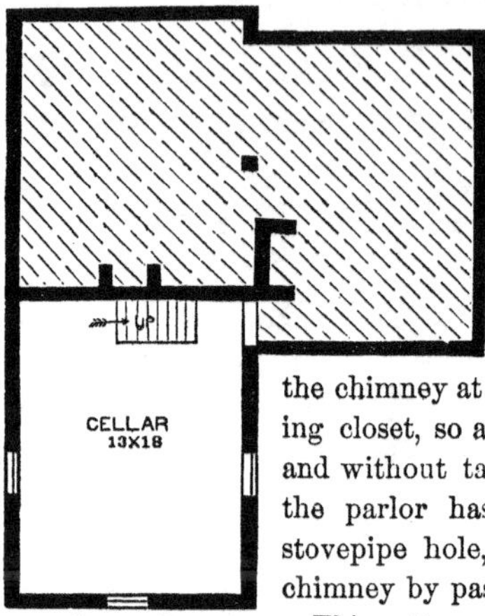

Cellar Plan.

The peculiar feature of this design is the *one* chimney, which answers for all the rooms. The flue of the kitchen fireplace is brought over to the chimney at the ceiling of the intervening closet, so as to be entirely out of sight and without taking away any room, and the parlor has a blind mantle with a stovepipe hole, connecting also with the chimney by passing under the stairs.

This cottage can be built for $595; or if inclosed with clear, narrow clap-boards, for about $16 more.

Fig. 23.

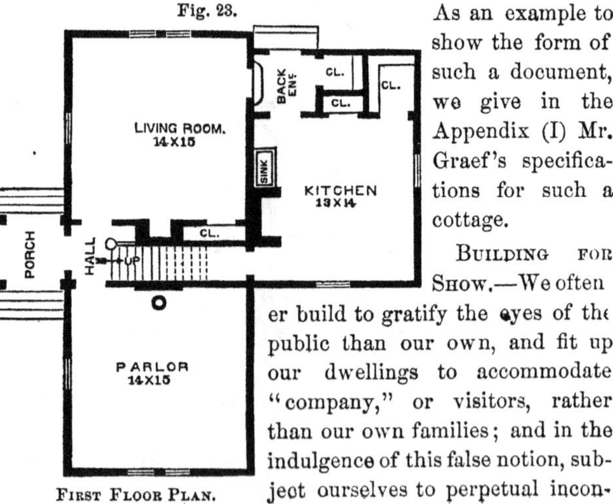

First Floor Plan.

As an example to show the form of such a document, we give in the Appendix (I) Mr. Graef's specifications for such a cottage.

Building for Show.—We oftener build to gratify the eyes of the public than our own, and fit up our dwellings to accommodate "company," or visitors, rather than our own families; and in the indulgence of this false notion, subject ourselves to perpetual inconvenience for the gratification of occasional hospitality, or ostentation.—*L. F. Allen.*

Fig. 24.

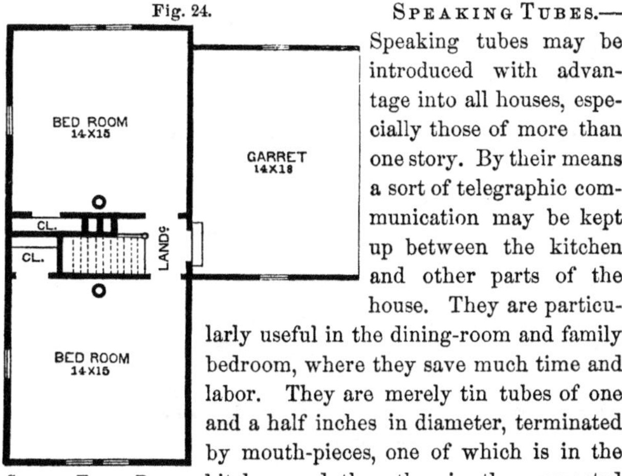

SECOND FLOOR PLAN.

SPEAKING TUBES.—Speaking tubes may be introduced with advantage into all houses, especially those of more than one story. By their means a sort of telegraphic communication may be kept up between the kitchen and other parts of the house. They are particularly useful in the dining-room and family bedroom, where they save much time and labor. They are merely tin tubes of one and a half inches in diameter, terminated by mouth-pieces, one of which is in the kitchen and the other in the connected apartment. Their cost is trifling.

IV.—AN ENGLISH COTTAGE PLAN.

The first-floor plan of this design is modified from one found

Fig. 25.

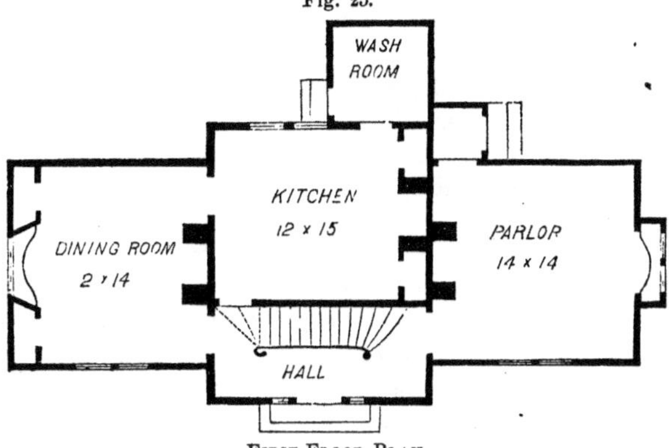

FIRST-FLOOR PLAN.

in Field's "Rural Architecture," and there said to be of English origin. It presents a compact arrangement of rooms, with no waste space, and admits a symmetrical elevation either in the pointed or in the Italian style, as may be desired. The number of angles in the outside walls, however, renders it considerably more expensive to build than a square house with equal interior accommodations. Many will consider the

Fig. 26.

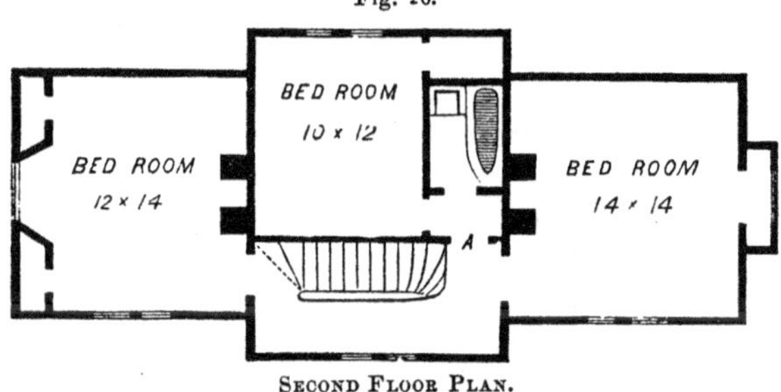

SECOND FLOOR PLAN.

superior beauty of such a building a full compensation for the extra expense.

The bath-rooom, on the second floor, is to be lighted by having the upper half of the door glazed with ground glass. The opening marked A is to be an arch. The kitchen flue is to be carried through the wall into the jamb of the adjoining bedroom fire-place. In the dining-room, and in the bedroom over it, closets are obtained, and the effect of a bay secured by recessing one of the windows, a method which may frequently be adopted with advantage.

V.—A SUBURBAN COTTAGE.

This design represents a small, but comfortable and convenient house for a family requiring but a moderate amount of space. As shown, it is better adapted for a village or suburban residence than for a farm-house, but with a little change in its plan would answer well for the latter.

Fig. 27.

PERSPECTIVE VIEW.

On the first floor an ample hall (7×13) furnishes access to a good-sized parlor (13×17) and a convenient kitchen (15×15)

Fig. 28.

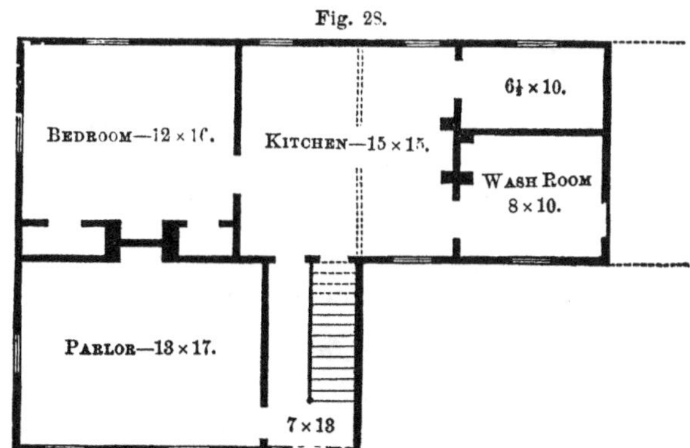

FIRST FLOOR PLAN.

(which will also serve as a dining-room), with a large pantry and a wash-room attached. On the other side of the kitchen or dining-room is a commodious family bedroom (12×15), with a fire-place and two large closets. The height of wall in this story is 8 feet.

Fig. 29.

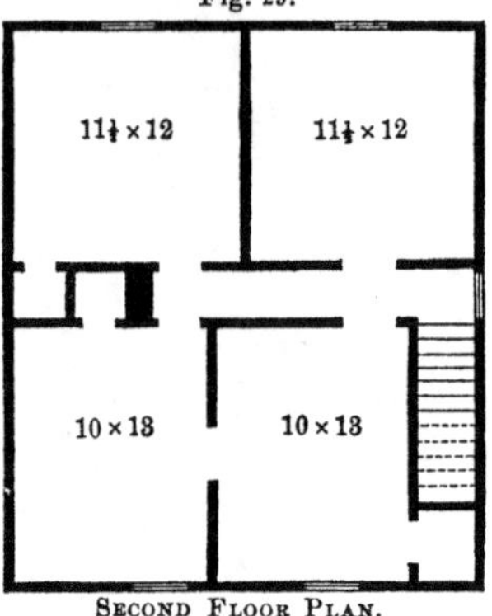

SECOND FLOOR PLAN.

The second, or attic, floor affords four good rooms, the walls rising four feet above the floor and the roof having a high pitch. The two front chambers communicate by a door, in order that they may be used in connection or separately, as may be desired. The two in the rear may be very prettily finished by arching the ceiling.

The cellar extends under the parlor and hall. It is 4½ feet excavation and 1½ above ground.

This house can be built of wood, in a plain but good and substantial manner, a hundred miles from New York, for about $800. It might be much improved by the addition of a bay window in the parlor and a veranda in front of the wing or ell part. If designed for a farm-house, the wing might be extended in the rear, so as to furnish the additional accommodations required. In short, this is a plan which can be adapted to circumstances. Its dimensions may be reduced to one story, rendering the cost less than our estimate, or it may be made two full stories in height with the same size of rooms, or larger ones, without at all interfering with the general arrangement.

VI.—A SMALL GOTHIC COTTAGE.*

This is another of Mr. Graef's designs, and shows an admirable arrangement of accommodations for a family of six or seven persons.

The rooms on the first floor may all be used in connection,

* F. E. Graef, Architect, 56 Wall Street, New York.

Fig. 30.

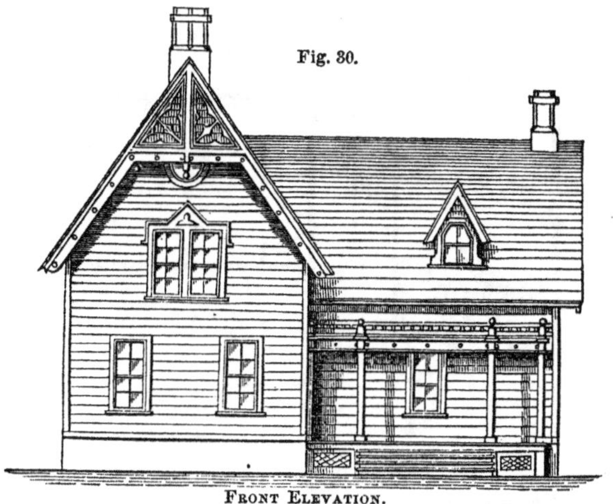

FRONT ELEVATION.

or each separately, as may be desired. Thus, if the kitchen be used as a dining-room also, as is often the case in houses like

Fig. 31.

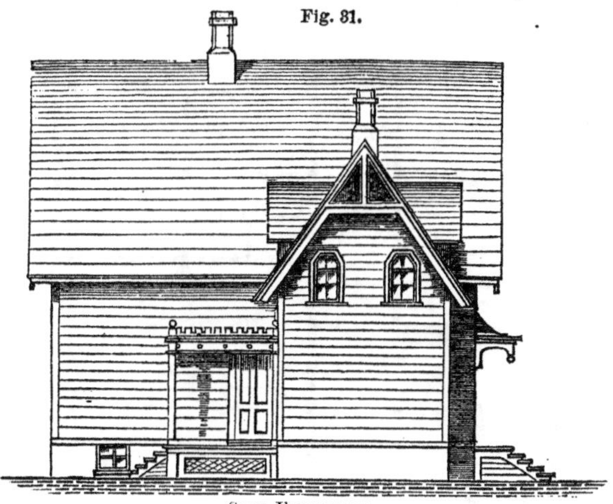

SIDE ELEVATION.

Fig. 32.

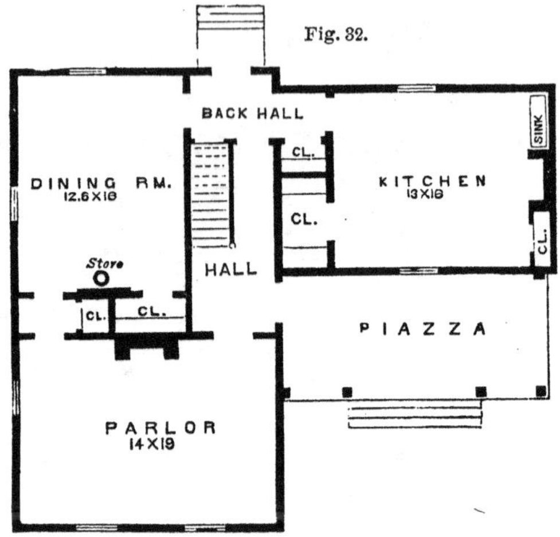

FIRST FLOOR PLAN.

this, the apartment designated as a dining-room may be used as the family bedroom.

Fig. 33.

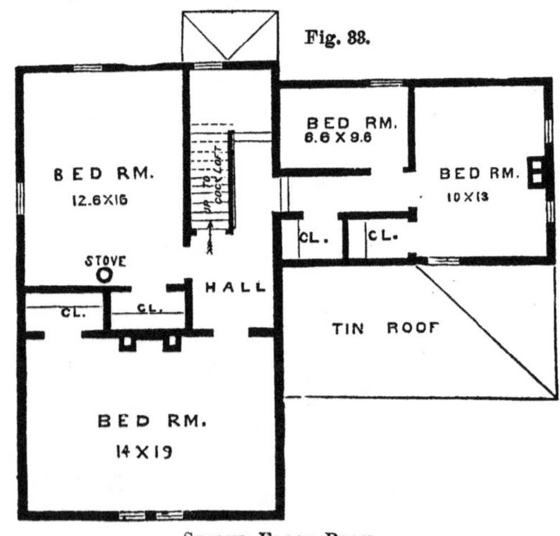

SECOND FLOOR PLAN.

If desirable, the two main bedrooms on the second floor may communicate in the same way as the parlor and dining-room below. There is a good-sized cock-loft of easy access, in which another small bedroom might be arranged.

This design, with dormer windows, veranda, hood over the back door, and tracery on the gables, as shown, can be executed for $1,125. The same ground plan, with elevations finished in a plain, bracketed style, without dormer windows, may be executed for $125 less.

ATTIC ROOMS.—All attic rooms, even in the plainest house, should be back-plastered between the rafters. This costs but little, and serves to render the rooms cooler in summer and warmer in winter than they otherwise would be.

ARCHITECTURAL FINERY.—"I am no advocate for meanness of private habitation. I would fain introduce into it all magnificence, care, and beauty, where they are possible; but I would not have that useless expense in unnoticed fineries or formalities; cornicings of ceilings and graining of doors, and fringing of curtains, and thousands such things, which have become foolishly and apathetically habitual—things on whose common appliance hang whole trades, to which there never yet belonged the blessing of giving one ray of real pleasure, or becoming of the remotest or most contemptible use—things which cause half the expense of life, and destroy more than half its comfort, manliness, respectability, freshness, and facility. I speak from experience; I know what it is to live in a cottage with a deal floor and roof, and a hearth of mica slate; and I know it to be in many respects healthier and happier than living between a Turkey carpet and gilded ceiling, besides a steel grate and polished fender."—*Ruskin.*

A NEW METHOD OF VENTILATION.—A syphon ventilator, applicable to the ventilation of houses, ships, etc., has lately been patented in England. The principle of the invention consists in creating, by means of a tube or shaft fixed in the roof of a building, two opposite currents, one of which carries off the impure air while the other introduces fresh air, the temperature being regulated by simple appliances in the shape of valves. This ventilator never permits the accumulation of foul air at the top of an apartment. In summer time, by opening the valves to the full extent, the temperature may be rendered the same within as without; while in winter time, the artificial heat, by means of fires or warming apparatus, of whatever nature, causes the impure air to ascend with such a degree of velocity that, by partially opening the valves, it is carried away very rapidly.

VII.—A SYMMETRICAL COTTAGE.

This is a house of greater pretension, in reference to style, and of higher cost than either of the preceding. Its symmet-

Fig. 34.

PERSPECTIVE VIEW.

rical form, handsome porch, and ample verandas give it an expression of elegance combined with convenience and comfort.

The various apartments on the first floor are compactly and conveniently arranged, each being accessible from the hall without passing through another. The dining-room, which may also be used as the common family sitting-room, is a good-sized and handsome apartment. The kitchen, without opening directly into the dining-room, is easy of access and convenient. It has liberal pantries or closets marked *c c* in the plan. If required for a farm-house, a lean-to might be cheaply added in the rear, affording a dairy-room, wash-room, and other needed accommodations. The parlor might be improved, at a moderate expense, by the addition of a bay window.

Fig. 35.

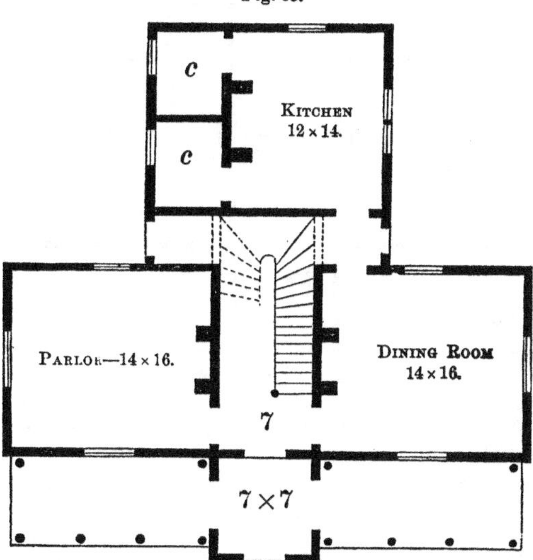

FIRST FLOOR PLAN.

On the second floor we have three bedrooms with closets; a bath-room and water-closet; and a small room over the porch, which would be a very pleasant summer apartment in which to work or read; or it might be used as a bedroom. The bath-room and rear bedroom are entered from the first landing of the stairs, this part of the house being two and a half feet lower than the front part.

The style of the elevation is that modification of the Gothic

Fig. 36.

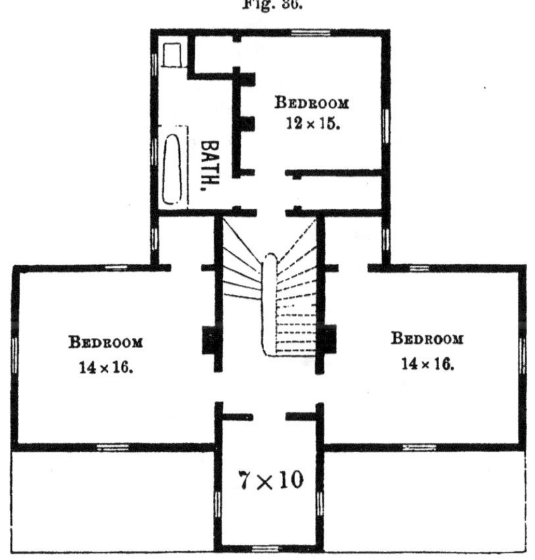

SECOND FLOOR PLAN.

which prevailed in England in the reign of James I. We are not aware that any examples of this style have yet been erected in this country.

A CEDAR CLOSET.—A closet or press for linens or woolens should, if practicable, be supplied with cedar shelves.

A SINK.—A sink on the second floor for the use of the chamber-maid, when it can be economically planned and rightly managed, is very convenient.

VIII.—A SEMI-SOUTHERN COTTAGE.

This is a house well adapted to the Middle and Southern States, although for the latter a veranda should be thrown

Fig. 37.

PERSPECTIVE VIEW.

around the front and sides. The design of the elevation is a borrowed one. The annexed plans were designed in adaptation to it by John Crumly, Architect, New York.

Fig. 38.

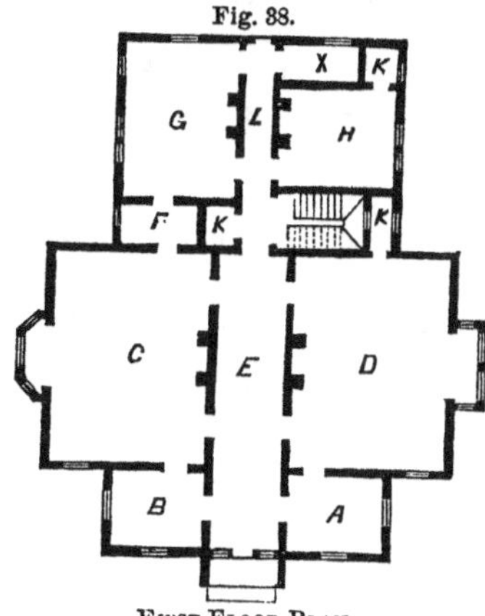

FIRST FLOOR PLAN.

A—Reception Room.... 9.0 × 11.6
B—Conservatory .... 9.0 × 11.6
C—Dining Room........18.0 × 25.0
D—Parlor..............18.0 × 25.0
E—Hall................ 8.6 wide.
F—Pantry.............. 5.0 × 9.0
G—Kitchen ....13.6 × 18.0
H—Breakfast Room.....11.0 × 13.6
I—Store Room......... 4.6 × 9.6
K—Closets .... 4.6 wide.
L—Back Hall...........

The two small rooms marked A and B, in the first-floor plan, which communicate so conveniently both with the hall and with the adjoining rooms, form a peculiar feature in this plan. In a village or suburban dwelling they may be made to minister to use as well as to beauty, whether their office may be such as we have indicated or not. The broad and unobstructed front hall, running quite through the main building, is expressive of breathing space, fresh air, and summer comfort, and forms a commodious ante-chamber to the rooms on each side. The kitchen (G) communicates with the dining-room (C) through the pantry (F) as well as by way of the back hall. The room marked A may be used for a bedroom, if not required for the purpose we have indicated.

Fig. 39.

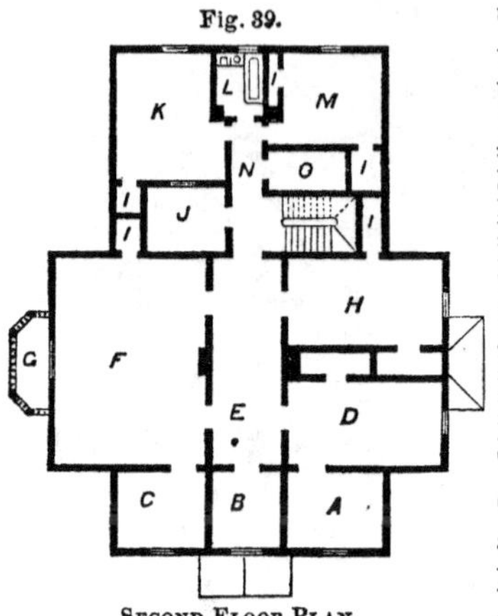

SECOND FLOOR PLAN.

A—Dressing Room... 9.0 × 11-0
B—Boudoir.. ...... 8.6 × 9.0
C—Dressing Room.... 9.0 × 11.6
D—Bed Room.........11.0 × 18.0
E—Hall .... 8.6 wide.
F—Bed Room.........18.0 × 25.0
G—Balcony...........
H—Bed Room........11.0 × 18.0
I—Closets.............
J—Cedar Closet.......
K—Bed Room.. .....13.6 × 15.0
L—Bath ....
M—Bed Rooms........11.6 × 13.6
N—Back Hall......... 4.6 wide.
O—Lumber Room .... 4.6 × 9.6

On the second floor we have an admirable arrangement of sleeping apartments, dressing-rooms, closets, and other accommodations.

These plans are on the scale of thirty-two feet to the inch.

HOUSES OF TWO STORIES.

> Here the architect
> Did not with curious skill a pile erect
> Of carved marble, touch, or porphyry,
> But built a house for hospitality.—*Carew.*

I.—A GOTHIC COTTAGE.

Fig. 10.

PERSPECTIVE VIEW.*

THIS handsome cottage very appropriately commences the chapter and connects it with the preceding; the center being two stories in height, and the wings only a story and a half.

Its two verandas, its fine bay windows, its balcony, its hand-

* Designed by John Crumly, Architect, New York.

some gable, and its grouped chimney stacks, give to this house an expression of simple elegance, combined with all the comfort and convenience that a cottage residence can well afford; and we are much deceived if this design do not prove a favorite among the patrons of our little manual.

Fig. 41.

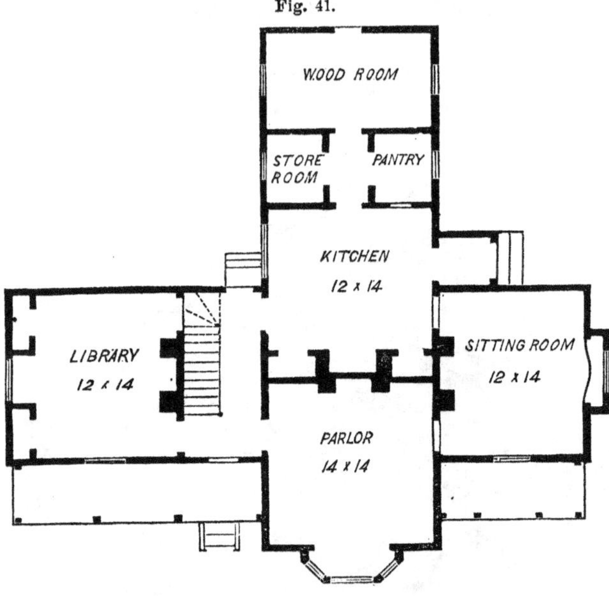

FIRST FLOOR PLAN.

The arrangement of the rooms on the first floor is compact and convenient. The parlor, although not large, is a very handsome apartment, and is conveniently connected with the sitting-room, so that the two can be used *en suite* if necessary. A door opening from the sitting-room into the porch may easily be had if desired, but would render the room somewhat colder in winter. The large room in the rear will serve as a wash-room, as well as a place for fuel. If the house should be built on a farm, the milk-room would occupy a part of the room just mentioned, the wood-shed being extended beyond.

On the second floor we have four fine sleeping-rooms and a bath-room, each with its separate entrance from a hall or passage. The front bedroom, with its fire-place and its balcony,

Fig. 42.

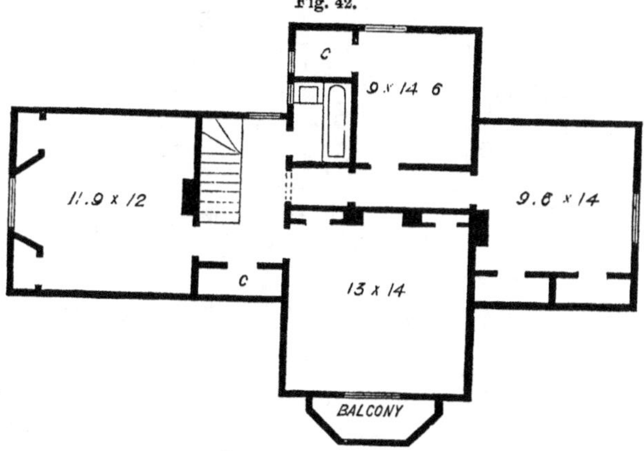

SECOND FLOOR PLAN.

is a particularly fine apartment. If it be desired to preserve the chimney projection, closets may be obtained by recessing the window, as in the case of the room at the left.

A cellar under the library and hall would be sufficient, unless it be built as a farm-house.

II.—A COUNTRY PARSONAGE.*

This design, with a few trifling alterations, has been executed for the use of a country clergyman, in which case the front room on the right hand was set apart for the study. It is equally adapted to the use of a layman.

Two-story frame houses, with accommodations such as this affords, and with handsome and substantial finish both out-

* F. E. Graef, Architect, 56 Wall Street, New York.

Fig. 43.

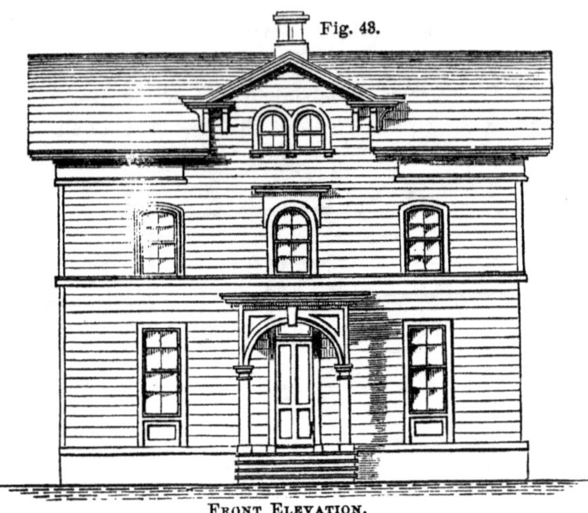

FRONT ELEVATION.

side and inside, can not generally be built for less than $3,000; but in this case the building committee applied to the architect

Fig. 44.

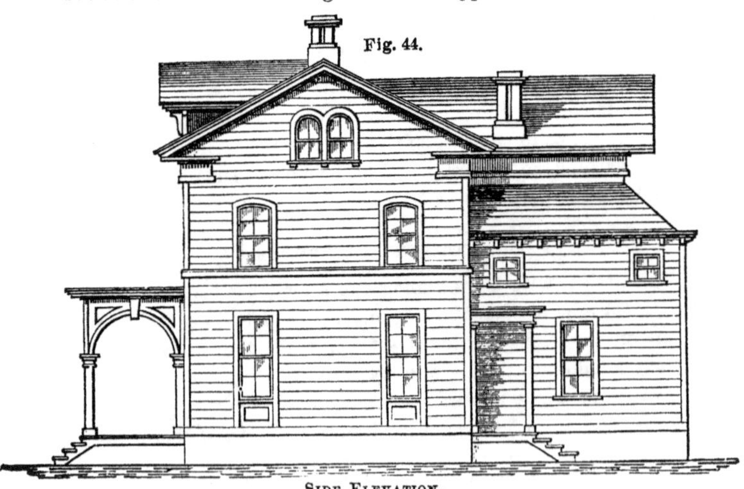

SIDE ELEVATION.

for plans and specifications for a house containing a parlor, a dining-room, a study or sitting-room, and liberal halls, stairs, and closets on the first floor; five rooms on the second floor; and a handsome outside appearance, the whole to cost not over $2,200. Here was a somewhat difficult problem. The accompanying plans and elevations show how successfully Mr.

Fig. 45.

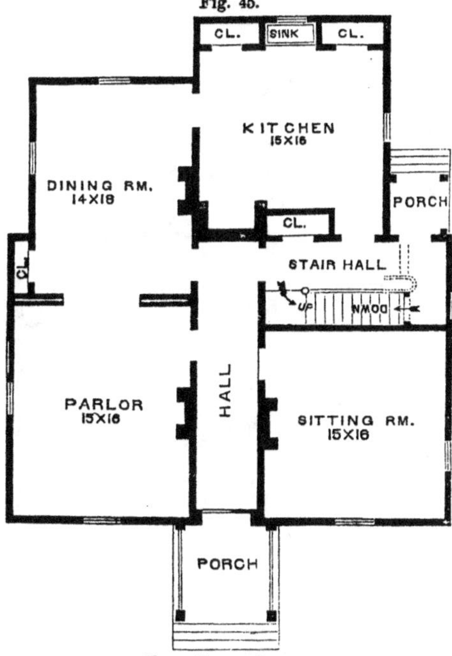

FIRST FLOOR PLAN.

Graef has solved it, the actual cost being but $50 over the sum named by the committee.

There is a large cellar under the house, with convenient access, both from the inside and the outside. Besides the rooms shown in the plans, two bedrooms might be had at a small expense in the well-lighted open garret.

All the materials used in the construction of this house are of approved quality. The frame is of strong pine and hemlock timber; the outside is inclosed with clear, narrow clap-boards; the roof is covered with cedar shingles, and painted; the floors are of 1½ inch mill-worked pine plank; the doors are 1½ inch thick, paneled, and furnished with mortice locks; all casings,

Fig. 46.

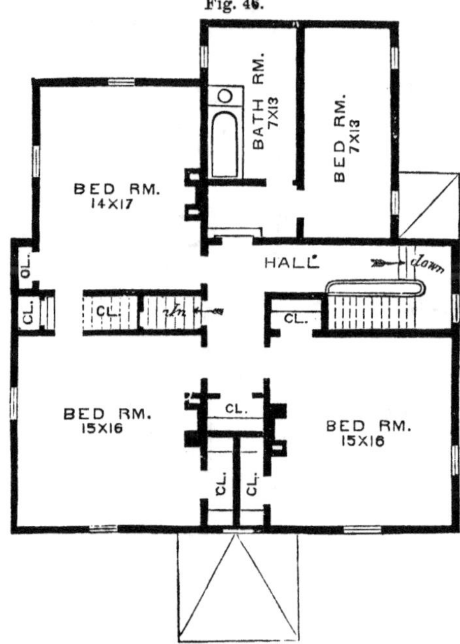

SECOND FLOOR PLAN.

inside and outside, are handsome, bold, and executed after working drawings; the windows are glazed with single, thick French glass; the parlor, dining-room, study, and front hall are hard finished and have molded cornices, and the other rooms, landings, etc., with the best brown wall. All outside studdings are back-plastered; the whole of the wood-work ordinarily painted is covered with two coats of zinc paint; the usual gas-pipes are put in; and the kitchen sink is supplied with water from the street.

We have been thus particular in reference to the materials and construction of this house, because, having been built, its actual cost is known, and will serve as a basis on which to calculate approximately the cost of other similar houses.*

III.—"FRUITLAND" COTTAGE.

The accompanying design represents a house erected at "Fruitland," near Augusta, Georgia, by D. Redmond, Esq., one of the editors of the *Southern Cultivator*. It is a concrete or

Fig. 47.

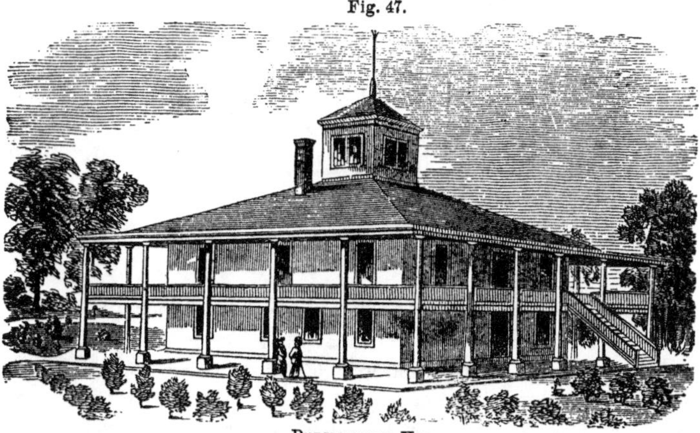

PERSPECTIVE VIEW.

gravel-wall building, and the mode of its construction may be found detailed in the Appendix. Mr. Redmond appends to the design the following remarks:

"The most obvious requirements of a Southern country house are—*ample space*, *shade*, and *ventilation*. Where land is

* Mr. Graef will be happy to furnish working drawings of this or any of his designs, should they be required.

abundant and cheap, the ground plan should be so extended as to get all the room needed as near the ground as possible, and avoid the fatiguing ascent of high flights of stairs. On any

Fig. 48.

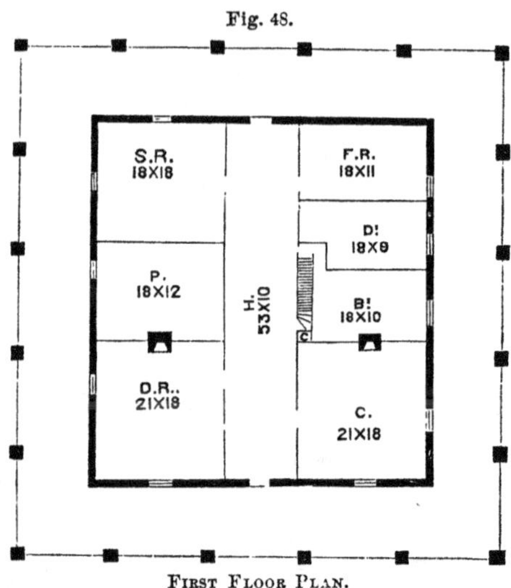

FIRST FLOOR PLAN.

H., hall, 58 x 10 feet; D. R., dining-room, 21 x 18; P., pantry, 18 x 12, adjoining the dining-room; S. R., store-room, 18 x 18, next to pantry; O., office; B., bath-room; D., dairy, 18 x 9; F. R., fruit-room.*

proper location, where the land is high, dry, and airy, a basement *entirely above the surface*, with one story above that, for parlor, sleeping-rooms, etc., will be found well adapted to the wants of a moderate family. Externally, the house should present a reasonable degree of architectural style, corresponding with the interior, and in harmony with the surrounding scenery. Thus, while a Swiss or Gothic cottage would be out of place in a low, level, and warm country—a flat-roofed Tus-

* For the ripening of pears, keeping of winter fruits, etc. When not used for the intended purpose, the latter room may serve as a general lumber-room, or a servant's bed-room.

can or Italian villa would be equally inappropriate amid the heavy snow-storms and wild tempests of the Alps. This sense of *fitness* should naturally lead us, in the erection of a country house for the South, to study carefully the peculiarities of our climate and surroundings, in addition to our own individual wants, and to modify existing modes into what some one has called the 'comfortable and convenient,' as distinguished from the merely 'ornamental' styles of architecture.

"The *site* of the house represented on page 79 is upon a pic-

Fig. 49.

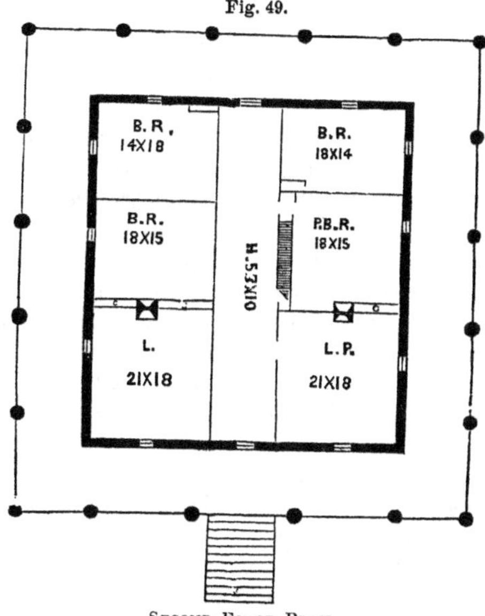

SECOND FLOOR PLAN.

H., hall, 53 × 10 feet; L., library, 21 × 18; B. R., B. R., B. R., three bedrooms, respectively 18 × 15, 18 × 14, and 18 × 11; P., parlor, 21 × 18; P. B. R., parlor bedroom, 18 × 15; c., c., c., closets.

turesque elevation in the orchard at 'Fruitland.' It is on the dividing ridge between Rae's Creek and the Savannah River, and from the peculiar formation of the locality commands a very beautiful prospect of the city of Augusta, the opposite hills of South Carolina, and the surrounding country.

"By reference to the elevation and accompanying plans, it will be seen that the house is a nearly square structure of two stories, fifty by fifty-five feet, entirely surrounded and shielded from sun and storm by an ample veranda, ten feet wide. This veranda is supported by twenty columns of solid pine, one foot in diameter, turned tapering, and bored entirely through lengthwise, to prevent outside shrinkage. These columns rest on square brick pillars, built up on concrete foundations. The lower story, or basement, contains the dining-room, pantry, store-room, office, bathing-room, fruit-room, and ice-house—in short, all the *working rooms*, or apartments for every-day practical use; while the second story contains the library, parlor, bedrooms, closets, etc. Two large halls, fifty-three by ten feet, run directly through the building, securing perfect ventilation. The second story has transom-lights over each door and opposite the outer windows, to admit the freest possible circulation of pure air. The basement floor is raised *several inches above the surface*, filled in with pounded rock and gravel, and laid in cement, which adheres firmly to the walls, thus affording perfect security against fire, dampness, and the depredations of rats and other vermin. The stairs leading from the basement to the second floor, and thence to the observatory or cupola, are removed to one side of their usual position in the halls, leaving the latter entirely free and unobstructed. The lower division walls, separating the hall from the dining-room, office, etc., are built of concrete, one foot thick, but all the partitions, above and below, are lathed and plastered. Two chimneys afford six fire-places, with flues for stove-pipes, etc. The windows are large, and so hung on springs that the upper sash can be let down and kept in a *fixed position*, for ventilating purposes. The roof is 'hipped,' or four-sided, and covered with the best cypress shingles."

IV.—S. H. MANN'S OCTAGON PLAN.

This plan was designed by Mr. S. H. Mann, of Beloit, Wis., and first appeared in the *Country Gentleman*, together with basement and chamber plans. We give this alone, as furnish-

Fig. 50.

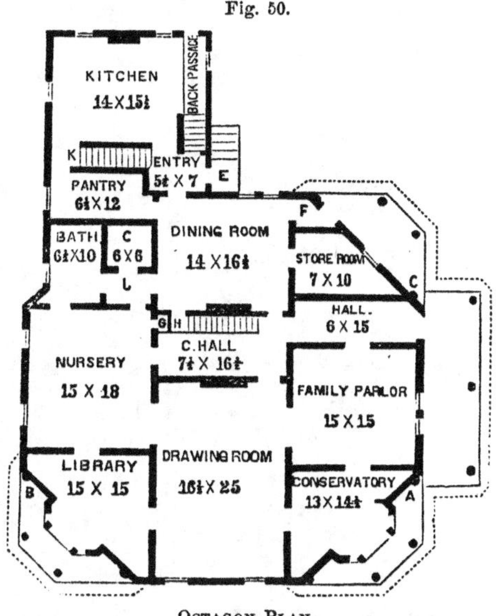

Octagon Plan.

ing hints, at least, toward the best possible arrangement of rooms within octagon walls, and giving the reader an opportunity to compare this form with the rectangular. Our individual opinion on the subject has already been expressed.

V.—A SOUTHERN HOUSE.

This design was made to meet the wants and tastes of a particular family, but will, we trust, be found, in its main features, to be equally well adapted to the use of many others. It is planned on a liberal and at the same time an economical scale the halls, stairs, veranda, arcade, balcony, etc., being

Fig. 51

A SOUTHERN HOUSE—PERSPECTIVE VIEW.

Fig. 52.

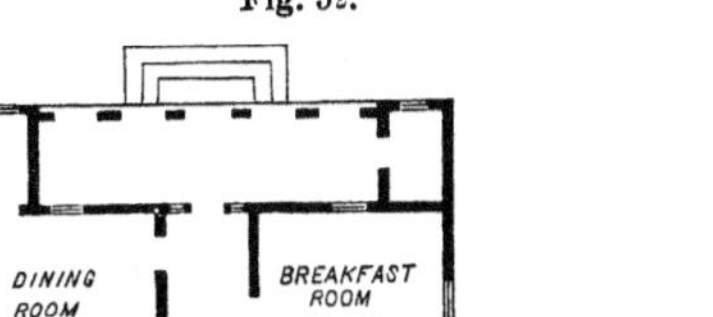

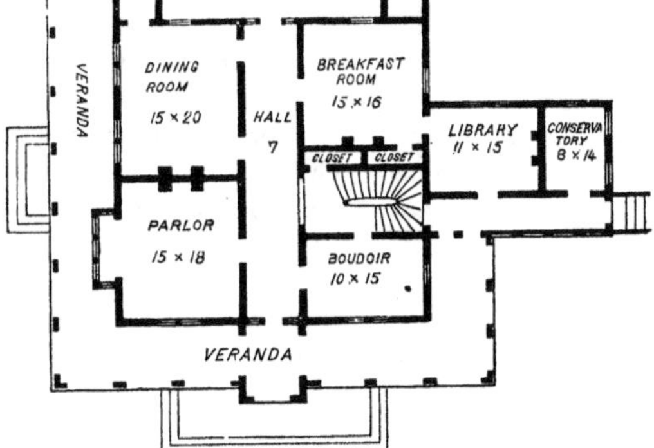

FIRST FLOOR PLAN.

spacious, to meet the requirements of a warm climate, while the rooms are of a moderate but comfortable size, and no waste of space is allowed. The plan may be easily modi-

Fig. 53.

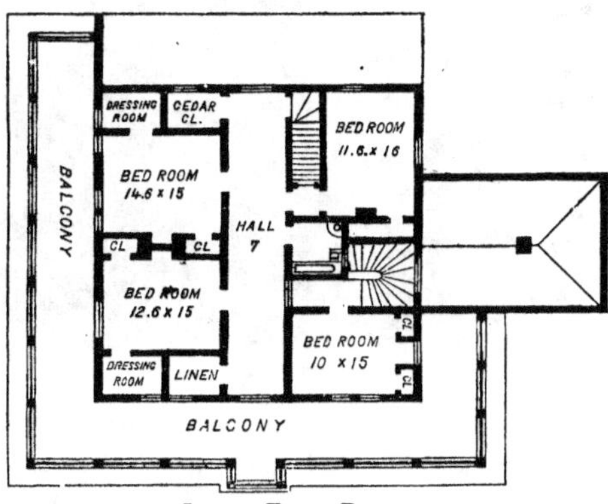

SECOND FLOOR PLAN.

fied by omitting the wing, carrying the veranda to the rear, and inclosing, if desired, the space now occupied by the arcade. The disposition of the various apartments on both floors was made with strict reference to comfort and convenience, and shows for itself in the plans.

The elevation is in the Italian style, with only such modifications as the necessities of climate and materials seem to render necessary, and presents a handsome and characteristic appearance. It was designed under our directions by Mr. John Crumly, Architect, of New York, who will furnish working drawings, specifications, etc., if desired.

VI.—A SQUARE COTTAGE.

The accompanying plans and elevation represent a medium-sized two-story house, so divided as to combine convenience

Fig. 54.

PERSPECTIVE VIEW.

with economy of space. The main part of the house is exactly square, giving more inclosed space for the amount of wall than any other rectangular form. A hall extends through the house, from which doors open from each room, thus securing a free circulation of air. The bow windows in the parlor and dining-room, as well as the verandas in front and rear, although very desirable, may be dispensed with if it be required to build for the smallest possible sum.

Fig. 55.

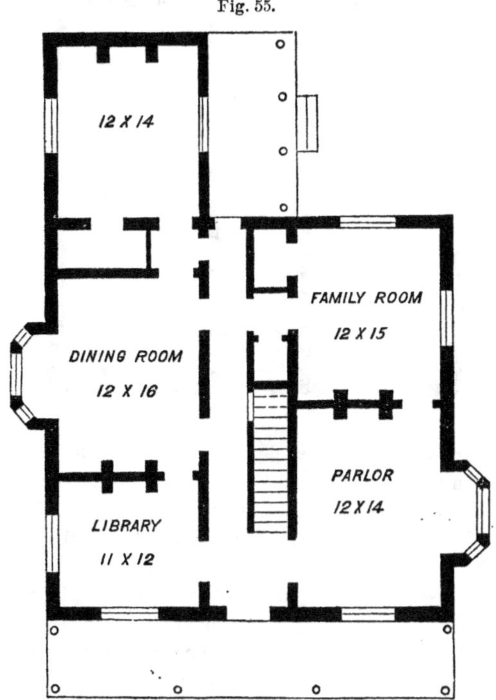

FIRST FLOOR PLAN.

On the first floor we have a parlor (12×17), a living-room (12×14), library (12×11), a dining-room (12×16), and, in the wing, a kitchen (12×14). If wanted for a farm-house, a dairy-room can be added to the kitchen.

On the second floor we have four large bedrooms, a large hall-closet, a bath-room, and a dressing-room. We have made the bedroom over the parlor a little irregular in shape, which allows two good closets to each room. If this irregularity be

Fig. 56.

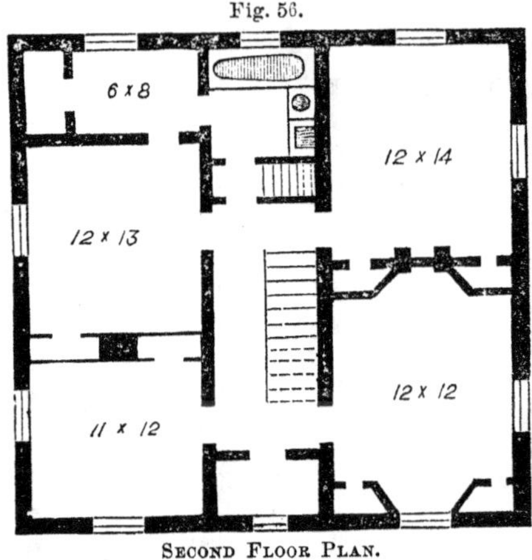

SECOND FLOOR PLAN.

objected to, a closet for each room may be obtained in the way shown for the rooms on the other side of the hall. Next to the bath-room are stairs leading to the attic or roof.

First story is to be 11 feet high; second story 10 feet high, clear. There is a cellar 6½ feet high under part of the house, with entrance to it under main stairs and outside entrance. Cellar walls and foundation are 12 inch brick walls, or 20 inch stone walls. It is inclosed with narrow, clear clap-boards. Cornices, caps, etc., to have a bold projection. Main roof to be covered with tin; kitchen roof to be covered with shingles. All rooms, landings, and closets are to be hard finished. Floors to be of mill-worked pine plank. All outside walls and second-story ceilings to be back-plastered. Room doors are 1½ inch thick; closet doors, 1¼ inch—all paneled. Inside casings to have back-bands and back-moldings, except to closets.

The estimated cost, including marble mantles to all fireplaces, but exclusive of plumbing work and gas-pipes, will not exceed $2,800. It may be built, however, with lower ceilings and plainer in and outside finish, without destroying in the least the general appearance, for $2,300.

VII.—A STONE COUNTRY HOUSE.

This design shows a house of rather more pretension than the last. The size and location of the rooms can be seen at a glance. The halls give access to every room without passing

Fig. 57.

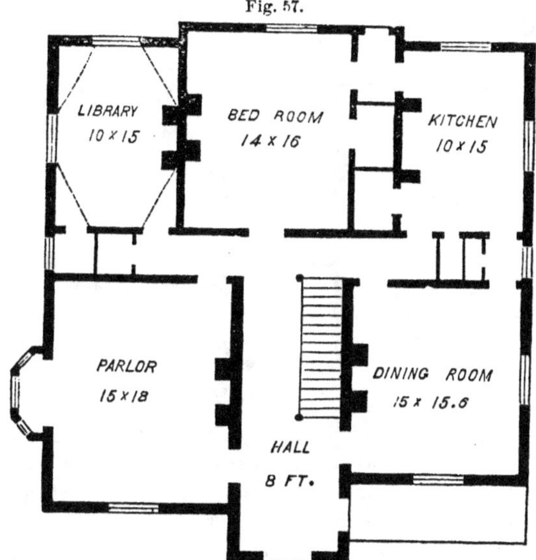

FIRST FLOOR PLAN.

through another. They are lighted by a window over the front door and by having the bedroom door half sash.

The second story has the same general plan as the first, giving five large bedrooms, a bath-room, and a fine small room in front hall. The stairs to the attic adjoin the back passage.

As persons may be differently situated, so they might desire some changes in the general plan, which can be easily made without interfering with the rest. A wing, projecting either

Fig. 58.

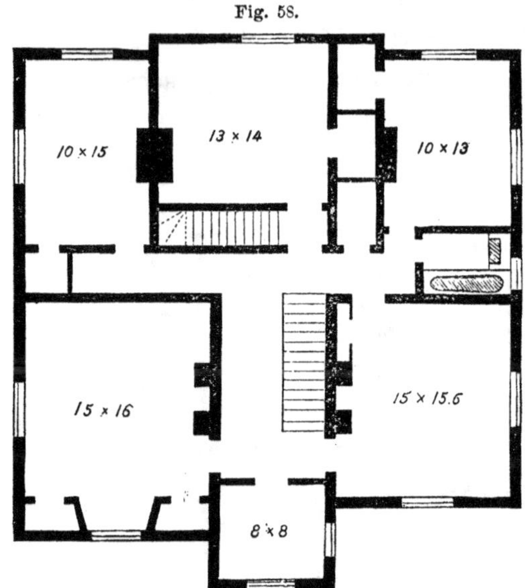

SECOND FLOOR PLAN.

to the rear or the side of the kitchen, for pantry, wash-room, dairy, or whatever may be needed, can be readily added. Some would prefer to make the library in an oval or octagonal style, as indicated by the dotted lines, with closets in the corner, dispensing with those in the hall.

Fig. 59 shows the perspective view.

This house is designed to be built of roughstone walls, neatly pointed, and have dressed blue or brown stone corners and dressings. The roof is covered with slates.

Fig. 59.—A Stone Country House—Perspective View.

VIII.—A CIRCULAR HOUSE.

There are queer people in the world—a great many of them—and it is not strange that there are also queer houses. Now, as our little book is made for everybody, it is but just that queer people and their houses should be represented in it.

Fig. 60.

PERSPECTIVE VIEW.

Very few persons, we presume, will desire to build a circular house, although it is the form, as geometry demonstrates, in which the greatest possible space may be inclosed by a given amount of wall; but for the oddity of the thing, or because economy of space may be secured, somebody may wish to do it, and look for a design to adopt or imitate. Here it is!

This circular house, in many respects quite original in its plan, was erected by Enoch Robinson, Esq., at Spring Hill, Somerville, Massachusetts. No timber was used in its construction. The walls are made of plank sawed on a circle of 40 feet (the diameter of the house), nailed together, one above the other, in regular courses. The windows are made of four large panes of glass, in a single sash, which slides up into the wall, entirely out of the way. The inside blinds are arranged in the same manner.

The oval parlor is 24 feet long by 15 feet wide. The circular library, opposite, is 13 feet in diameter, leaving a fine front entry between these two curves. The kitchen, next the circular library, has a slate floor and walls of varnished whitewood. Between the kitchen and the large dining-room is the

Fig. 61.

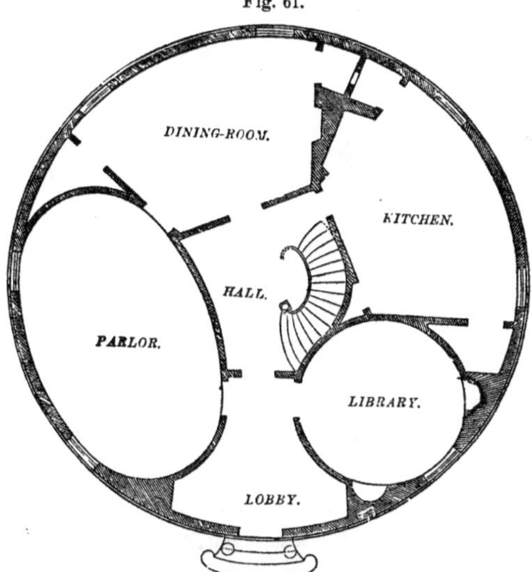

FIRST FLOOR PLAN.

chimney and the kitchen and dining-room closets, so arranged as to occupy very little room.

On the second floor are seven chambers, two of them quite large, all opening into a pleasant rotunda, 13 feet in diameter, beneath the central skylight.

The accompanying sketch and plans will give a good idea of the general appearance and arrangement of this truly original and unique edifice.

Though made of the best materials, and of superior workmanship, this building was erected at an expense much less than that of a square house erected in the ordinary way.

Fig. 62.

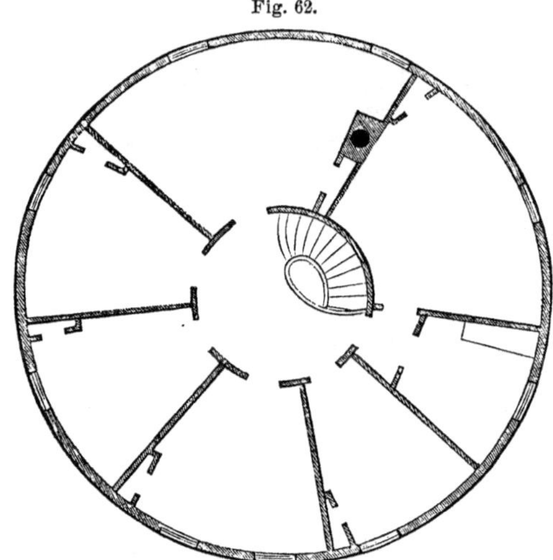

SECOND FLOOR PLAN.

ORNAMENTING THE ROOF.—A good effect is produced on the steep roofs of Gothic houses by cutting the shingles in certain patterns before laying them. One of the simplest forms is made by cutting the end of each shingle to a point, so as to form a diamond pattern when laid. The shingles must be of good quality and uniform width and thickness. These ornamental shingles may also be used with good effect instead of boards, for the outside covering of wooden cottages, forming a warm and durable wall.

IX.—A SWISS COTTAGE.*

This design, like most others representing cottages and houses in the Swiss style, and intended for execution in this country, lacks some of the peculiarities of the genuine Swiss cottage, as it is seen in Switzerland. Both the external finish and the internal arrangements are necessarily modified, to adapt them to our climate and habits. The architect has, therefore, aimed to retain the general character of the style merely,

Fig. 63.

PERSPECTIVE VIEW.

and to produce an effect as little removed from that of the original *chalêt* as the circumstances permit.

The plans require little explanation. A cottage of the dimensions of this ought to have both front and back stairs, but to save expense we have made one flight serve in this case. The front entrance is into a lobby, from which both the parlor and the dining-room are entered. These rooms also open into the stair hall, which is conveniently placed for daily use, and from which the kitchen is entered. The latter has also a separate entrance, from the outside, through the sink-room. A cellar under a part of the house would be sufficient.

---

* F. E. Graef, Architect, 56 Wall Street, New York.

This design, executed in wood, will cost, according to the architect's estimate, $2,300. Foundation or cellar walls to be either stone sixteen inches thick, or of brick eight inches thick;

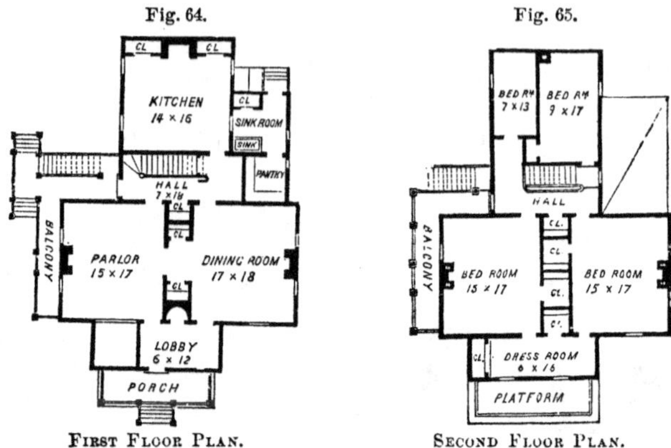

Fig. 64. FIRST FLOOR PLAN.

Fig. 65. SECOND FLOOR PLAN.

first-story rooms and landings to be hard finished; second-floor rooms and landings to be brown wall for papering; inclosing to be done with clap-boards; roof to be tinned. The ground plans must be reversed, to agree with the perspective view.

SERVANTS' BEDROOMS.—These are generally, and for obvious reasons, placed in the attic (where there is one); but, where it can be so arranged, it is well to have a bedroom opening out of the kitchen, or of easy access from it, for the person whose duty it is to be last in that apartment at night and first in the morning. It saves many steps.

IMPORTANCE OF ARRANGEMENT.—A great deal of labor, especially of women, is saved by an economical arrangement of the more common rooms; and hundreds of miles in walking, in the aggregate, avoided annually by a few feet of lessened distance between the principal points.—*J. J. Thomas.*

X.—A DOUBLE COTTAGE*

On account of the economy thus secured, it is sometimes desirable to build two distinct dwellings under one roof. This arrangement saves not only part of the material but all the exterior covering and finish of two walls; and as three sides are still open to the light and air, no serious disadvantage need arise from their exclusion on the other side. Such houses, however, must be skillfully planned in order to avoid dark and

Fig. 66.

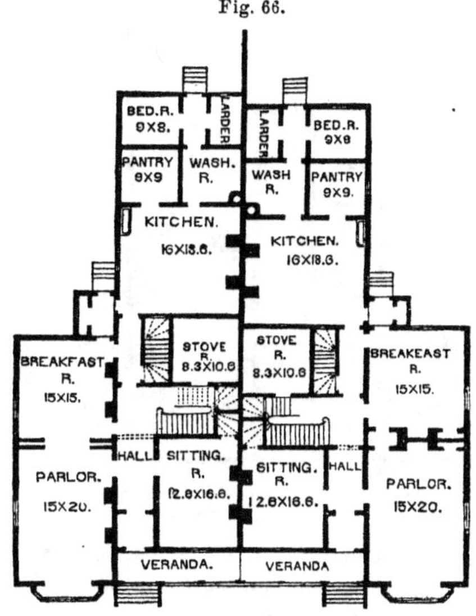

FIRST FLOOR PLAN.

badly ventilated rooms. The acompanying design, we think, meets the requirements of such a house in a very satisfactory manner, and is offered with confidence to persons desiring to build two dwellings in one.

It will be seen that the two houses, although similar in their general features, are considerably varied in their details. We

* John Crumly, Architect, New York.

find the same rooms in each, but their sizes, forms, and relations to each other are different. For instance, on one side we have the parlor and breakfast-room arranged *en suite*, with sliding doors between them, while on the other they merely communicate by means of common doors. The sitting-rooms also differ in form and size, and so on. This gives persons purposing to adopt such a design a choice of plans, as

Fig. 67.

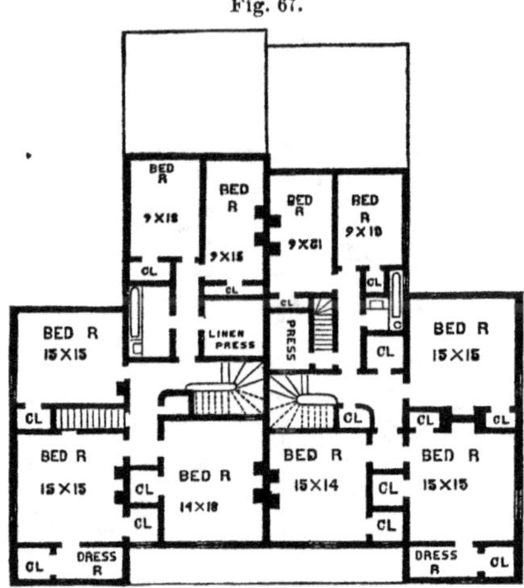

SECOND FLOOR PLAN.

both houses may be built like the right-hand plan, both like the left-hand plan, or each differing from the other, as shown. The two houses afford a fine front, and may have a handsome elevation in such a style as may be preferred.

As a general thing, however, we think double houses not desirable, and that all that is saved in the expense of erection is more than paid for by the inconvenience of having neighbors so near. Nearly all houses in cities, it is true, are built so close as a double house; but in cities there are no such things as neighbors, and families live in adjoining houses for years without any acquaintance.

VI.

FARM-HOUSES.

Between broad fields of wheat and corn,
Is the lowly home where I was born;
The peach-tree leans against the wall,
And the woodbine wanders over all.—*T. B. Read.*

I.—PRELIMINARY REMARKS.

CONVENIENCE and comfort are the first requirements of a farm-house; but there is no reason here, more than in any other sort of residence, why regard should not be had to beauty of external features. The farmer may properly have as handsome a house as the village lawyer or doctor, and in its general features it need not differ widely from that of either. It is mainly its adjuncts—its barns, stables, piggery, poultry-house, and other out-buildings—that give the residence of the agriculturist its peculiar appearance. Almost any of our designs, with slight modifications—mainly the enlargement of the kitchen and its offices, the addition of a milk-room, etc.—may be adapted to the uses of a farm-house. For this reason we content ourselves with giving two or three houses planned with special reference to the farm.

Permanency should characterize the farm-house, therefore we should be glad to see brick and stone brought into more general use in the construction of such buildings. Rough stone is an admirable material for a farm-house and may often be advantageously used. Concrete, too, in favorable situations, and with due regard to the essential conditions already mentioned (in Chapter II.), may be adopted with profit, instead of wood. But whatever the material may be, let the construction be substantial and enduring.

"The kitchen," some one has said, "is the heart of the farm-house." Let it receive a large share of attention in your plan. See that it is large; well lighted; well ventilated; provided with a large pantry, a sink, etc., and convenient of access. Domestic help is not generally abundant in the farmer's family. Too much labor, at best, devolves upon the mistress. We should have reference to labor-saving, then, in every arrangement. To these ends we hope our plan will furnish useful hints.

II.—A MODEL FARM-HOUSE.*

This design is presented by the architect as a model farm-house, suitable for a farmer in easy circumstances and with the taste and culture which should accompany such a con-

Fig. 68.

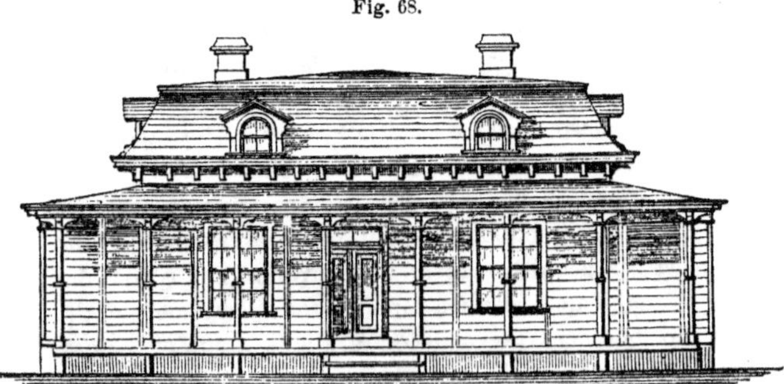

FRONT ELEVATION.

dition in life. For less expensive farm-houses, almost any of our cottage designs, with slight alterations, will serve.

* F. E. Graef, Architect, 56 Wall Street, New York.

The prominent features of this design are its great extent on the ground, compared with that of the second story; compactness in the arrangement of the rooms; and the comparative

Fig. 69.

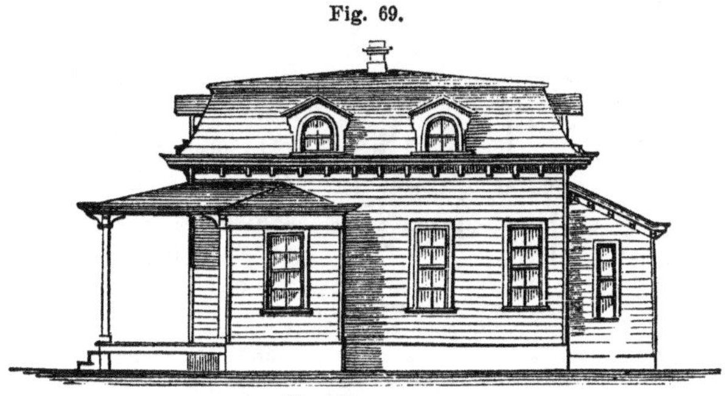

SIDE ELEVATION.

prominence given to the kitchen and its offices; all of which promote the saving of labor and indicate adaptation to the uses of a farm-house.

The front hall and back hall, with their respective entrances, are separated, so that the front hall, parlor, family bedroom, or sitting-room (according to the use which may be made of it), may always be kept clean and free from unnecessary contact with the every-day work of the house; while the back hall serves for all the common uses of the household. At the same time the ventilation and coolness of the whole in summer is secured by opening the door by which the halls communicate. The kitchen, dairy, and other domestic offices, it will be seen, are admirably situ-

Fig. 70.

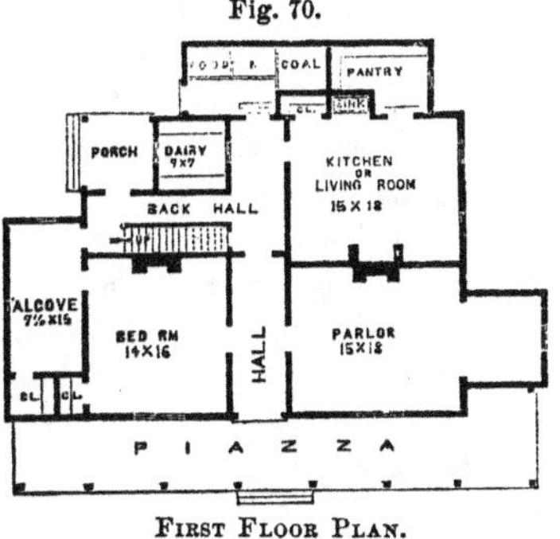

FIRST FLOOR PLAN.

ated in reference to the back hall and entrance. The second or attic floor affords four bedrooms, all of which are provided with large closets, and may be warmed.

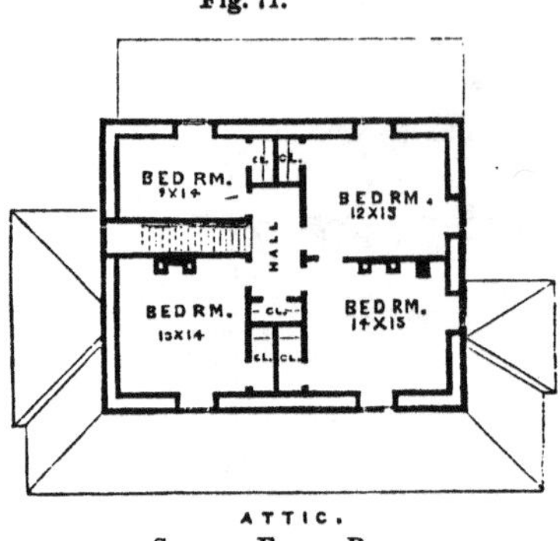

Fig. 71.

SECOND FLOOR PLAN.

The exterior presents a decidedly rural appearance, and indicates the character of the house at a glance. Its veranda, porch, bay window, and curved roof with dormer windows, give it an expression by no means commonplace and quite picturesque.

Executed in wood, and finished throughout in a substantial and liberal style, and with a cellar under the whole, this house will cost $2,250. It is also very suitable for execution in stone or brick.

III.—A FARM-HOUSE PLAN.

This plan, in its general features, is borrowed from Lewis F. Allen's excellent work on "Farm-Houses, Cottages, etc.," but is so modified in most of its details that it would not be just to hold Mr. Allen responsible for any fault it may contain.

In this plan, as in the previous one, the front hall is separated from the back hall by a door, to shut out, when occasion requires, all the sights and sounds of the kitchen from the parlor and living-room. The living or family-room is a large apartment, and will serve as a dining-room when the kitchen, which in farm-houses is generally used for this purpose, may prove too small, or be otherwise occupied. These two rooms may be made to communicate by means of a door where the closet is represented in the design. We have dispensed with the back stairs, which are, however, very desirable, and may be had in the back hall by making it a little wider at the expense of the bedroom, or by omitting the store-room. Connected with the kitchen fire-place is an oven, which, in our humble opinion, no cooking stove or range yet invented renders useless. In the wing, the pantry, milk-room, wash-room, bath-room, and privy are conveniently arranged. Beyond these, and separated from them by the wood-shed, are the piggery, workshop, stable, etc.

Fig. 72.

FIRST FLOOR PLAN.

The main building should be two stories in height, and the wing a story and a half. We omit a second floor plan, which may easily be arranged from this, which we give rather as a hint or suggestion than as a finished design.

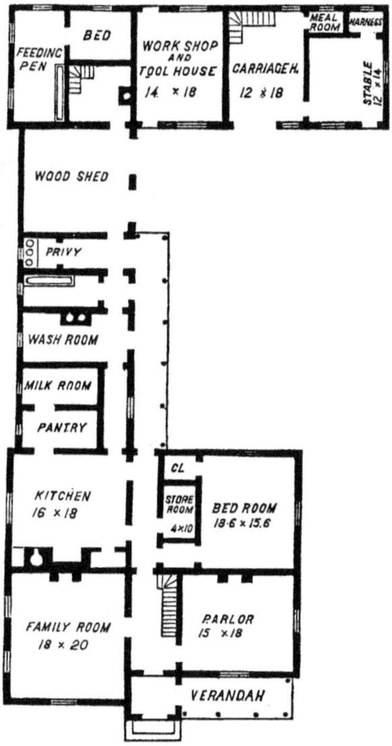

OLD ROOFS.—Whenever a roof begins to leak, and you wish to re-shingle it, do not take off the old shingles—put the new shingles on top of the old ones—but make use of six-penny nails in place of four-penny or shingle nails. The advantage of this method will consist in the following particulars:

1. Will save the expense of removing the shingles.
2. The building will not be exposed to wet in case of rain before it is finished.

3. The roof will be much warmer and tighter.

4. Neither snow nor rain can beat under the butts of the shingles by heavy winds.

5. The roof will last full one third longer.

I have tried this plan, and find that it has these advantages: It takes no more shingles, no more nails in number—only a little longer—and no more time to put them on, and if done in a workmanlike manner, it will look as well as if single. But it should be done before the old shingles are too much decayed.

All the moss—if any—should be removed or swept off with a stiff broom before putting on the new shingles.—*National Era.*

VII.

VILLAS.

Here no state chambers in long line unfold,
Bright with broad mirrors, rough with fretted gold,
Yet modest ornament with use combined
Attracts the eye to exercise the mind.

I.—WHAT IS A VILLA?

HISTORICALLY, the question is readily answered. It was originally a summer residence in the vicinity of an Italian city, erected for occupation merely during the warm season. The word is now used with a wider signification.

According to Downing, "what we mean by a villa in the United States, is the country house of a person of competence or wealth sufficient to build and maintain it with some taste and elegance—the most refined home of America—the home of its most leisurely and educated class of citizens."

"What, then," continues Mr. Downing, "should the villa be architecturally? . . . . . . It should be, firstly, the most convenient—secondly, the most truthful or significant—and thirdly, the most beautiful, of dwellings.

"The villa should indeed be a private house where beauty, taste, and moral culture are at home. In the fine outlines of the whole edifice, either dignified, graceful, or picturesque; in the spacious or varied verandas, arcades, and windows; in the select forms of windows, chimney-tops, cornices, the artistic feeling has full play: while in the arrangement of spacious apartments, especially the devotion of a part to a library or cabinet, sacred to books, and in that elevated order and system of the whole plan, indicative of the inner domestic life, we find the development of the intellectual and moral nature, which characterizes the most cultivated families in their country houses."

II.—A SMALL VILLA IN THE ITALIAN STYLE.*

This, although not a large house, is planned on a more liberal scale, and betokens more expensive tastes, than any of

Fig. 73.

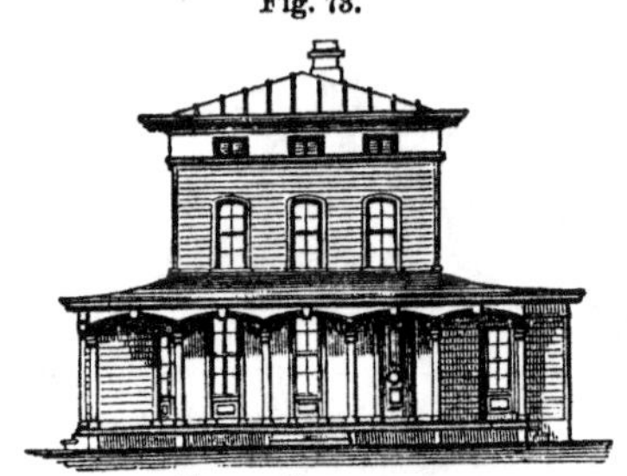

FRONT ELEVATION.

the designs hitherto given. The convenient access to all the rooms; their arrangement in connection with each other and

Fig. 74.

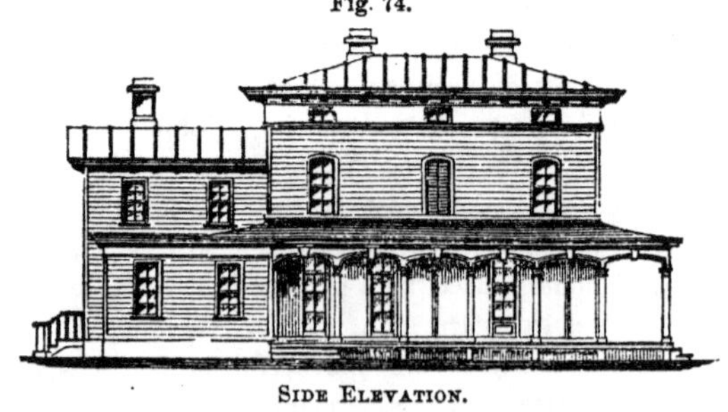

SIDE ELEVATION.

* F. E. Graef, Architect, 56 Wall Street, New York.

Fig. 75.

Fig. 76.

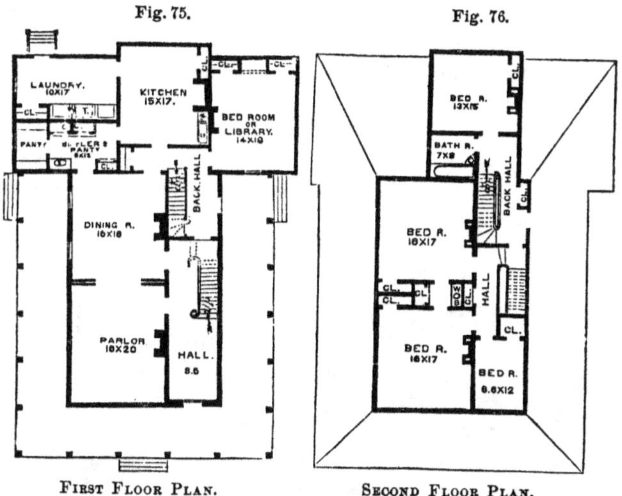

FIRST FLOOR PLAN. SECOND FLOOR PLAN.

with the halls; and especially the location of the kitchen in reference to the dining-room, butler's pantry, laundry, back-hall, etc., show a nice appreciation of the wants of a family of some wealth and cultivation as well as of the principles of economy in household labor. The spacious front hall, and the back hall with the separate stairs for the domestics, add to the characteristic features of the interior.

Fig. 77.

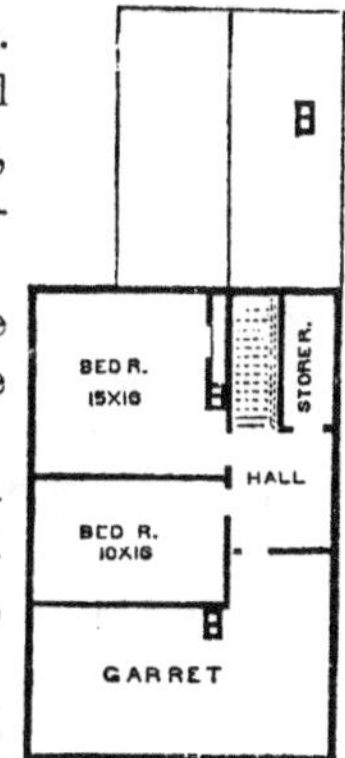

ATTIC PLAN.

The second and attic floors furnish ample bedroom accommodations, etc., for a large family. They require no explanation.

In its external form the house is well proportioned, and presents a pleasing appearance, its most striking feature being its fine veranda.

A design similar to this has been executed at Elizabeth, New Jersey, at a cost of about

$3,450, the whole being finished in first-class style. It may be built in a plainer way for from $400 to $500 less.

The scale in this design is reduced to thirty-two feet to the inch.

III.—A BRICK VILLA.

This may safely be pronounced a model design. Its great merits will be conceded by every one who will take the pains to examine it closely.

Fig. 78.

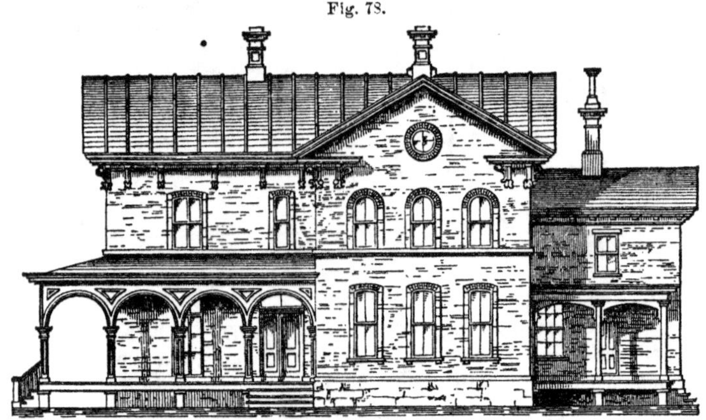

SIDE ELEVATION.*

On the first floor two opposite main entrances, with lobbies, give access to a fine vestibule in connection with the main stair-hall. This hall and vestibule are so placed as to afford direct access to a parlor, dining-room, sitting-room, and kitchen; and there being a fire-place in the vestibule, it will be seen at a glance how parlor, dining-room, and sitting-room may be used together whenever occasion may require. The dining-room and kitchen communicate through a butler's pantry. The library may, if desirable, have an outside entrance from the veranda in front of the kitchen.

---

* F. E. Graef, Architect, 56 Wall Street, New York.

The arrangement of apartments on the second floor is admirable. Each bedroom has a separate entrance from the hall, and, if desired, all of these in the main house may communicate with each other. The ceiling of the kitchen wing is

Fig. 79. Fig 80.

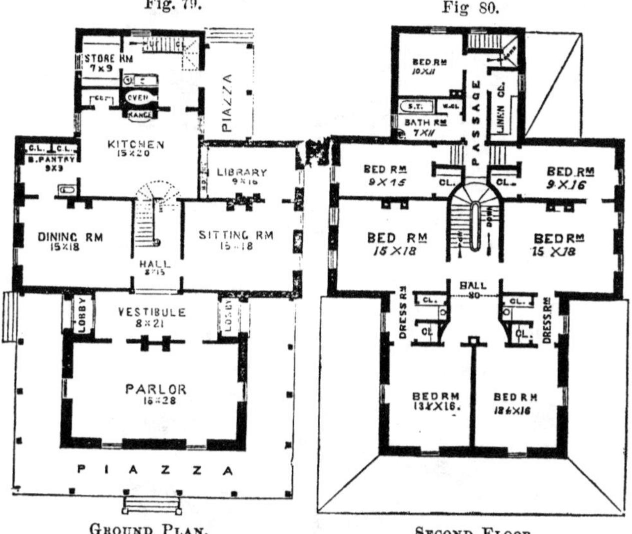

GROUND PLAN. SECOND FLOOR.

lower than that of the main house, which accounts for the stairs or steps shown in the plan; but this does not show in the first-floor ceiling. The main stairs are carried up to the attic, and lighted from above; besides, there is sufficient light for the second-story hall and passage, from a window at the end of the latter.

In the first design (fig. 81) the walls and all the dressings, except the window sills, are of faced-brick painted, with white mortar or dark stone putty. The roofs are of tin ornamented with tin rolls. There are inside shutters to all the windows in the main house.

The ceilings of the main house are 12½ feet high for the first

Fig. 81.

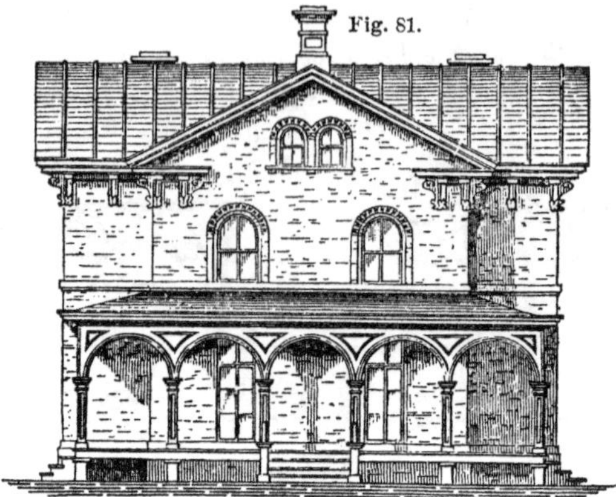

FRONT ELEVATION—No. 1.

story, and 10½ feet for the second story. Those of kitchen wing are 9½ feet and 9 feet respectively. Executed in a liberal

Fig. 82.

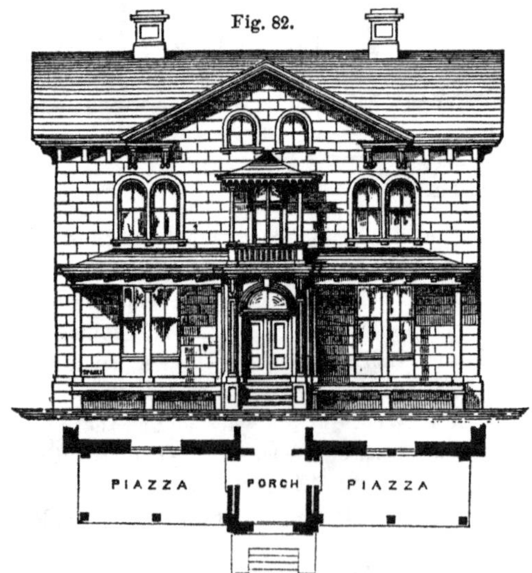

FRONT ELEVATION—No. 2.

style of inside finish, the cost will not exceed $9,000, including furnace, gas-pipes, plumbing work, and marble mantles.

Fig. 82 represents a front elevation of the same house with the parlor and vestibule omitted. A slight alteration in the design will admit of these being afterward added, bringing the house into the form represented in the previous design. As here shown, it makes a convenient but smaller house.

This design is intended to be executed in good hard brick, cemented on the surface, laid out in courses and painted. Although some architects vehemently protest against this so-called mastic wall, it is to be recommended for suburban houses of moderate pretensions, if the work be performed the right way.*

The cost of this house will not exceed $6,900, all included.

IV.—A GOTHIC VILLA.†

This house is entered through a low porch, of which the principal feature is three pointed arches supported on four octangular columns. This porch leads to a hall, 9.6×13.6, and from which doors open into—1st, a library on the right, 16×16, which is converted from a square into an octagon by cutting off the corners in the manner shown, thereby obtaining four closets for books; 2d, a parlor on the left, 16.6 × 18, having a bold, projecting window in front; 3d, a dining-room behind the library, 17×17.3, lighted by a bay window, semi-octangular on the plan, and furnished with a small

Fig. 83.

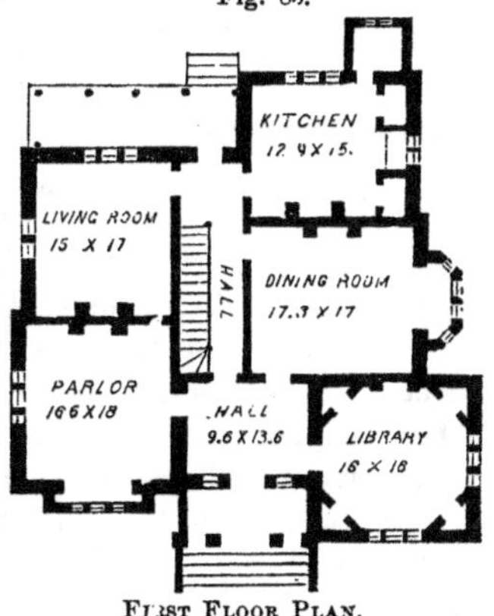

FIRST FLOOR PLAN.

---

* We quote Mr. Graef's description. Our own opinion of outside plastering, etc., has been expressed in Chapter II.

† J. Crumly, from a sketch by the author.

closet, for plate, taken off the kitchen; and, 4th, a staircase, terminating in a back entrance which opens upon a veranda. Two other doors lead from the staircase; one to a living-room on the left, 15×17, and the other to a kitchen on the right, 12.9×15, having a pantry, between which and the dining-room closet a very convenient recess is obtained, opposite one of the windows, for the table; a small store-room is provided behind, and is entered from the kitchen.

The following accommodation is obtained upon the chamber story, viz., a closet at the top of the landing, which may be used as a linen press; a bedroom, 15×15, over the living-room, with a closet; a bath-room, a bedroom 12.3 × 14, and a closet attached, over the dining-room; a nursery, 16 × 16, over the library; a boudoir, 9.6 × 13.6, over the hall, which leads to a balcony over the porch; and two bedrooms over the parlor, each of which is furnished with a closet.

Fig. 84.

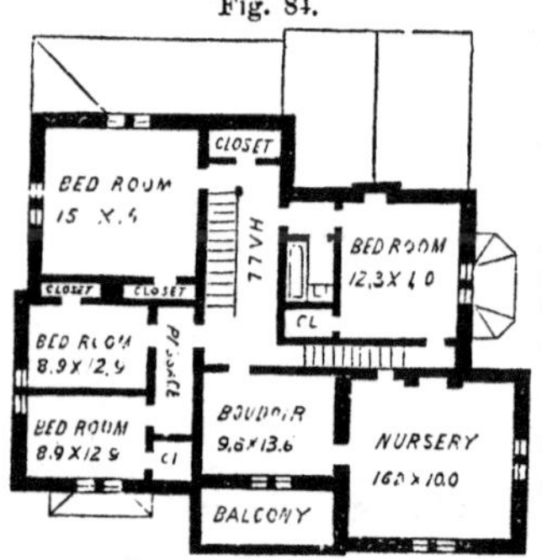

SECOND FLOOR PLAN.

The stairs leading to the tower are situated immediately behind the nursery, and an additional closet may be formed under the stairs, if thought necessary. The nursery may be formed into an octangular shape, if preferred, and four closets obtained, as in the library.

There are fire-places provided to the nursery and to the bedroom over the dining-room; there may also be fire-places obtained for two of the remaining bedrooms, namely, that over the living-room and the adjoining one over the parlor; these, in the present arrangement, it is proposed to heat by means of flues, and for this purpose the flues from below are gathered into one shaft between the closets.

The style is the English rural Gothic of the fifteenth century.

Fig. 85.—A Gothic Villa—Perspective View.

The quoins, window-dressings, porch, coping to side walls and gables, shields, mullions to windows, covers to projecting windows, embrasures and supporting brackets to tower, should be of roughly chiseled stone, and the remainder of the external work of rough stone, hammer dressed, but not laid in courses. The outer walls should be about twenty inches thick; the inner walls may be of brick, eight inches thick.

It may perhaps not be unnecessary to say that it is useless to attempt this style of building in wood; the quaintly antique and massive character of the architecture can not be obtained otherwise than in stone, and any attempt to produce it in timber will only result in a caricature, and be so much time and money thrown away. It may also be added, that this style will not admit of external shutters of any kind; whatever may be needed in this way must therefore be fixed inside.

V.—A PICTURESQUE VILLA.

We insert, as we have before had occasion to remark, some very queer houses, and some which by no means commend themselves to our individual taste and judgment, because we make this book for all sorts of people—the queer ones with the rest—and must tolerate all tastes and opinions while freely expressing our own. So we give this villa, which does not please us, with the hope that it will please somebody else. It was designed by Mr. Bradbury, of this city. The following is his description:

"This building is supposed to have grown gradually from a log cabin to its present comfortable proportions. The proprietor, we will suppose, goes into the Western wilds and selects a beautiful site, and (having, of course, consulted a member of that profession which demands as much study as 'law' or 'medicine') builds his (12×20 feet) cabin, which, for decency's sake, we will suppose to contain two apartments, a 'parlor-kitchen' (K.—10×10) and a bedroom (W.—10×8), afterward used as a kitchen and wash-room. In the course of a few years he adds the little bedroom (Pn.—7×6) and staircase (S.—7×12).

Fig. 86.—A Picturesque Villa—Perspective View.

afterward used as a pantry and back staircase. The girls now have a snug room to themselves, while the boys find a more

Fig. 87.

commodious dormitory in the loft. The house now presents the exterior of fig. 87. In the course of a dozen years the country around becomes settled. There is a brick-kiln and saw-mill near by. Railroads have cheapened other building materials, and increased the profitableness of his crops. "His family has been increased by

"Troops of tow-heads, bobbing in the corn."

They and the progress of civilization call for an enlargement of his habitation, which he builds according to the original plan (fig. 88), the old house now serving as a pantry (Pn.), kitchen

Fig. 88.

PERSPECTIVE VIEW.

(K.), washroom (W.), and back staircase. His house is now comprised in the entrance hall (L. H.—12×12), square drawing-room (H.—18×18), circular staircase (C. S.—12×12), the dining-room (Dn.—12×18), into which the winter bedroom (R.—12 × 12) opens, by folding doors, so that they can be made one at any time (and make one long dining-room when the house is further enlarged). He may throw out a bay win-

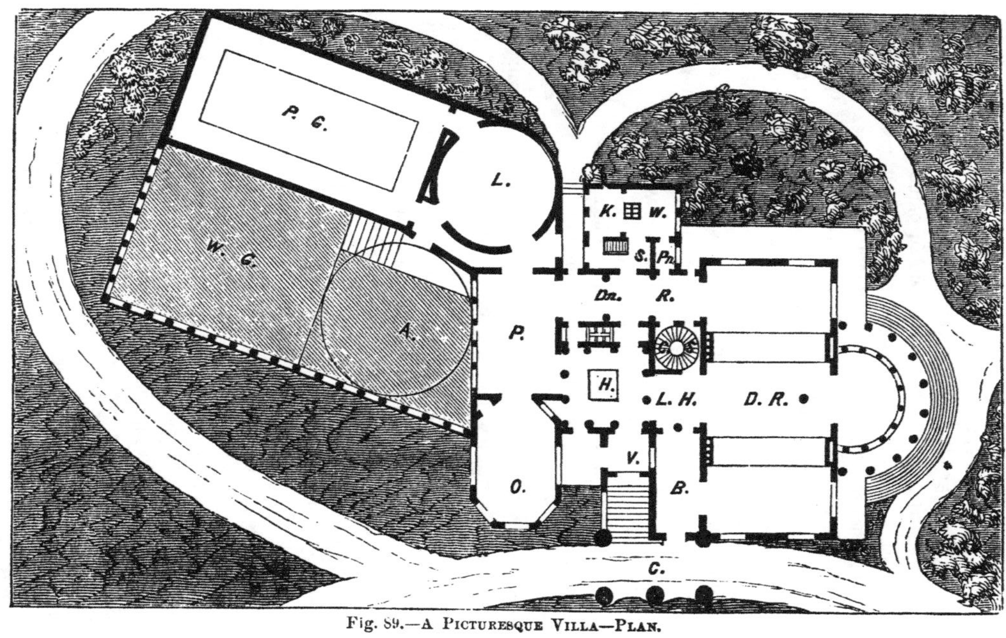

Fig. 89.—A Picturesque Villa—Plan.

dow here or a piazza there, or even the large drawing-room (D. R.—60×25), large enough to hold half the village; but the house with these additions satisfies him for years.

"His sons get into successful business in the neighboring city; his daughters are well married and have 'been abroad,' and they all insist upon adding the coach porch (C.), the cabinet (O., octagonal—18×24), the family drawing-room (P.—18×30), the library (L., circular, 30 feet across), the picture gallery (P. G., lighted from the roof—30×60, or more), and the aviary, grapery, or winter garden (W. G.), and upon making the square drawing-room (H.) a grand entrance hall open to roof, with galleries leading to the various chambers, provision for which has been made in framing the floors.

"The house or villa now consists of the grand entrance hall (H.), with its vestibules and coach porch; the large drawing-room (D. R.), with its accessory boudoir (B.), piazzas, bays, and balconies; the dining-room (Dn. R.), with its closets, pantry, kitchen, etc.; the small drawing-room (P.), the library (L.), the picture gallery (P. G.), the winter garden (W. G.), and the cabinet (O.). The upper stories are conveniently divided into chambers, dressing-rooms, bath-rooms, corridors, etc."

VI.—A SOUTHERN VILLA.*

This house consists of a large center and two wings, connected by two covered arcades of one story each. It is entered under a veranda 12 feet wide, which extends the whole length of the front, and is also continued around each side of the projecting portion of the center. The entrance door leads to an elliptical vestibule, 10×17, having four niches for statuettes, vases, etc. The vestibule opens on the right into a parlor, 17×21, and on the left into a drawing-room of a like size. Each of these rooms is lighted by two windows, of which those at the ends of the rooms are projecting. The vestibule at its farther end leads into a hall 8 feet wide, which extends across the whole

* J. Crumly, from a sketch by the author.

Fig. 90.—Southern Villa—Perspective View.

central portion of the building, and being continued outside of the center at each end so far as to embrace the veranda, terminates in an open arcade which leads to the wings. The center and wings at the rear of the building are also connected by two open arcades in the manner shown. Passing across the hall, we find the principal stairs, consisting of three flights —a central flight leading to the first landing, and two return flights, one on each side of the central, each of which return or side flights lands upon the chamber floor. The staircase is 14.6×17, and the entrance to it may be richly ornamented by means of two pilasters or columns supporting an arch above. Passing on toward the rear of the building under the first

Fig. 91.

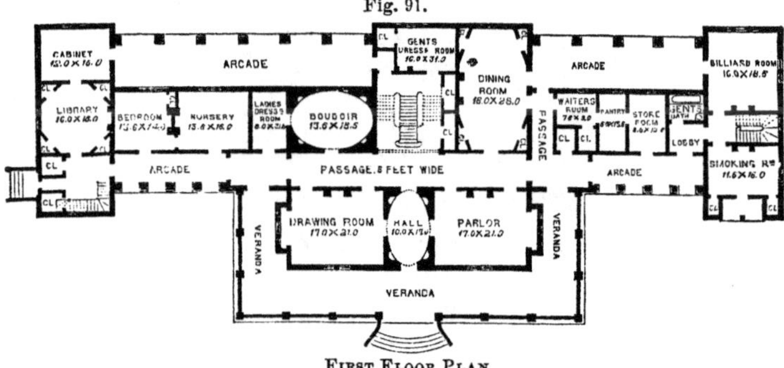

FIRST FLOOR PLAN.

landing of the stairs, we find two closets to the right, and under the first landing a door leading to a gentleman's dressing-room, 10×12.6, with closet attached; and at the opposite side of the landing we find a door opening upon a lobby which leads to one of the arcades at the rear of the building, before noticed. Returning to the hall, and proceeding along it to the right of the principal entrance, we find a dining-room, 16×28, lighted by a large window at one end; it is octangular in form, and by making it of this shape, four closets are obtained at the angles, as shown. This room has three doors, one opening upon one of the arcades at the rear, another opening to a passage which communicates with the waiter's room, and the third opening to the hall. The waiter's room is 7.6×9, and communicates with—a small closet; a pantry, 6×13.6; and a store-room, 8.6×13.6; the store-room has also a door into the front arcade. Continuing our progress along the arcade, we find, immediately after passing the store-room, a lobby which leads to a gentleman's bath-room, and also communicates with a staircase in the right wing of the building. Two doors open at the bottom of this staircase—one to a billiard-room, 16×18.6, at the rear of the wing, having a closet under the stairs before alluded to, and with a door opening upon one of the rear arcades; the other door at the bottom of the stairs leads to a smoking room, 11.6×16, which has also a door communicating with the arcade in front. Two closets are attached to the smoking-room, with a door between opening upon a platform occupying the space between the closets, extending to the front of the wing, and covered so as to form an open recessed space from the front wall of the wing, which admits of smoking in the open air.

Proceeding again along the hall, but to the left of the principal entrance, we come to a boudoir, 13.6×8.6, elliptical on plan, with four niches as in the vestibule, and for similar purposes; the boudoir opens into a lady's dressing-room, 8×13.6, which last is also entered from the hall. Succeeding this is a nursery, 13.6×16, communicating with a bedroom, 13.6×14, which is also entered from the arcade. The arcade terminates at the remaining or left wing of the building, with which it communicates by a door which leads into a large lobby, containing the stairs to the chamber floor, and two closets, between which is a side entrance door. This lobby leads to an octangular library, 16×16, which communicates with a cabinet, 12×16, from which a door opens to the left arcade at the rear of the building.

The second or chamber story is divided as follows: two triangular spaces are taken off the second landing of the principal stairs, in such a manner as to preserve the symmetry;

the landing is thus converted into a semi-octagon, and this process, in conjunction with that of narrowing the hall to five feet, enables us to obtain a number of closets, which are appropriated as shown on the plan. The entrance from this landing to the hall may be ornamented in a manner somewhat similar to the lower entrance before described.

A passage commencing at the landing on the dining-room side, leads to two bedrooms over the dining-room, that next the passage being 13.6×15, and the other 15×16; these may be made of equal size, if preferred; each has a closet attached. The passage turns at right angles, leads to a linen press, and terminates at a lady's bath-room. Bedrooms are also obtained over the parlor and drawing-room, each 16×17.6 and over the

Fig. 92.

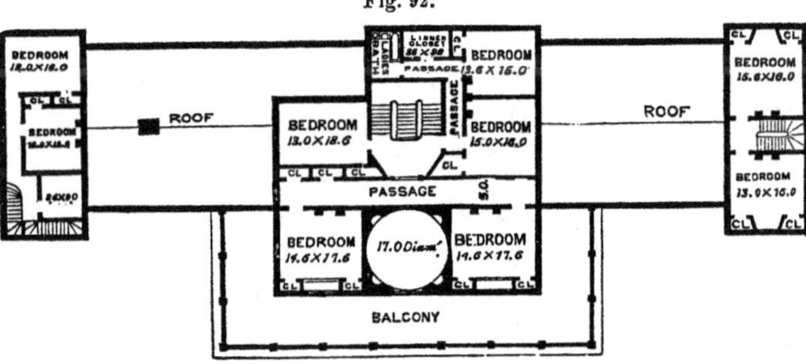

SECOND FLOOR PLAN.

boudoir, 13×18.6. All these bedrooms have closets attached, leaving two closets opening from the passage, unattached to any bedroom, and which may be applied to whatever purpose may be thought advisable. A circular room, 17 feet diameter, is located over the vestibule; this room, with a circular table in the center, covered with rare shells, bijouterie, etc., and with statuettes or vases in the niches, may be made to assume a very rich and ornamental character.

The windows to the parlor and drawing-room, to the bedrooms over them, and to the circular room, should be French casements opening to the floor, so as to allow access to the veranda and balcony.

Two bedrooms are also obtained over the billiard and smoking rooms; the former 15.6×15, and the latter 13×15, with closets to each; and two more bedrooms, with attached closets, and an additional large closet, are provided over the library and cabinet; that over the library being 12×13.6, and that over the cabinet 12×13. The stairs to the tower are situated along the external wall of the building, over the two closets before mentioned, as shown on the plan.

Access to the flat on the roof may be obtained by a step-ladder, which may be removed when not in use; or, what is still better, a flight of stairs may be constructed in the space occupied by the two closets adjacent to the bedroom over the boudoir, and inclosed by a door so arranged as not to interfere with the symmetrical appearance of the hall. Should this latter method be adopted, two or three bedrooms may be formed in the roof, and lighted by skylights from the flat.

The style is Italian. The quoins, the window and door dressings, the chimney tops, and the arcades are proposed to be of stone; the remainder of the external walls of good, square, well-burned brick. The quoins and window dressings to the first story are to be of the kind of work commonly known as rock-work; that is to say, the stones are to be first hammer-dressed, then truly bedded and jointed, and lastly a margin draft chiseled off the outer edges of the external surfaces; this draft should be about two inches wide, leaving the remainder of the external faces rough from the hammer. It is also proposed to execute part of the mason work of the arcades and of the wings in this style; but the portions of the elevation in which it is proposed to introduce this description of stone-cutting are sufficiently indicated on the engraving. The quoins and dressings to the second story are to project from the face of the brick-work, and to have the angles chamfered off. A good idea of the remaining features of the elevation will, it is presumed, be obtained from the engraving.

Fig. 93.—An Octagon Villa—Perspective View.

VII.—AN OCTAGON VILLA.

The main body of this house is a regular octagon on the plan, each side being 20 feet, giving the whole width of the main house 48 feet; with 12 feet additional for the wings. Rectangular apartments are built against four of the walls, forming four projections, each of which is 18.8×10, clear dimensions. The principal building—that is, the octagon—is two stories high, and the wings one story. The whole structure,

Fig. 94.

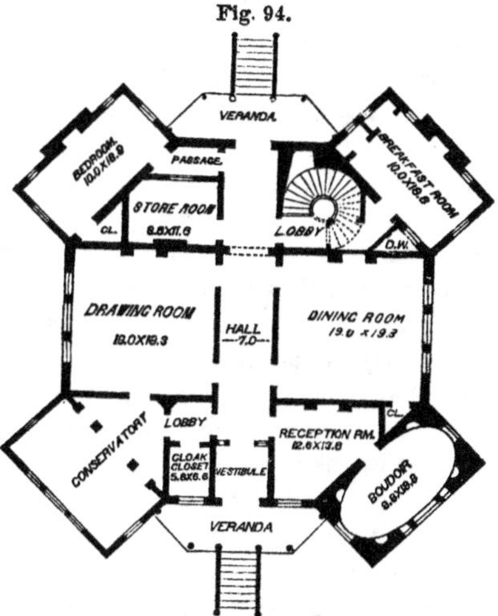

FIRST FLOOR PLAN.

for the purpose of giving effect to the elevation, is raised about six feet above the adjoining ground.

A flight of steps in front lands upon a veranda six feet wide, from which we enter through the front door to a vestibule, 7×7, and from which, passing through a glass door, we enter the hall, seven feet wide, which is continued through the building, having the rear entrance door at its farther extremity. Immediately inside of the glass door we find a door on each side of the hall; that to the right opens into a small, irregularly-shaped reception-room, of which the length inside, measuring across the fire-place, is 13.6; and parallel to the hall, 12.6. This room leads into an elliptical boudoir, 10×18.8, with niches in the walls. The door on the opposite side of the hall leads to a lobby, from which we enter into a cloak-closet 5×6; and going forward through the opposite door, we find ourselves in the conservatory. This room is also irregular in form, but notwithstanding its irregularity, a slight glance will show that it is symmetrical. The wall of the main building, which cuts it into two unequal portions, is perforated so as to allow of the introduction of Gothic columns and arches; and it is proposed not only to have the arches open, but also the spandrels between, and the whole of the space above to the ceiling; these perforations will, of course, be molded, and cusps, foils, and other Gothic ornaments introduced; creeping plants may be trained around the columns and through the openings, and if the ornamentation be of that light and graceful character of which the Gothic supplies such a variety, a very pleasing and picturesque effect may be produced. Proceeding along the hall, we find two doors opening into the drawing-room on the left, and also two doors opening into the dining-room on the right; each of these rooms is 19×19.3; the former opens also into the conservatory; the latter has a small closet attached for plate. Proceeding farther along the hall, we find the stairs to the right, and enter the breakfast-room from a passage formed under the upper landing; a door from this passage opens to the basement stairs, leading to the kitchen and other offices below. The breakfast-room is 10×16.3, and is fitted up with two closets; it has also a fire-place projecting outward, which may be made an ornamental feature in the elevation. On the other side of the hall we find a passage leading to a bedroom, 10×18.8, having also a projecting fire-place and a small closet. A door opens from this passage into a store-room. At the rear of the building another veranda is found, with a flight of steps as at the front.

Ascending the stairs, we enter a bedroom on the landing,

13×19.3, and passing forward we find a bath to the right, 7×7, and still farther we find two bedroom doors, one of which leads to an irregular-shaped room, being over the store-room and passage on the principal floor; the other, over the drawing-room, is the same size as that already described, 13×19.3—each of these bedrooms is provided with a closet. If a greater number of rooms be desired, these principal bedrooms can be divided in the manner shown by the dotted lines. It is supposed the servant's bedrooms will be in the basement. Opposite the bath-room door we find a door leading to an octangular picture-gallery, 19.3×19.3, from which, on the opposite

Fig. 95.

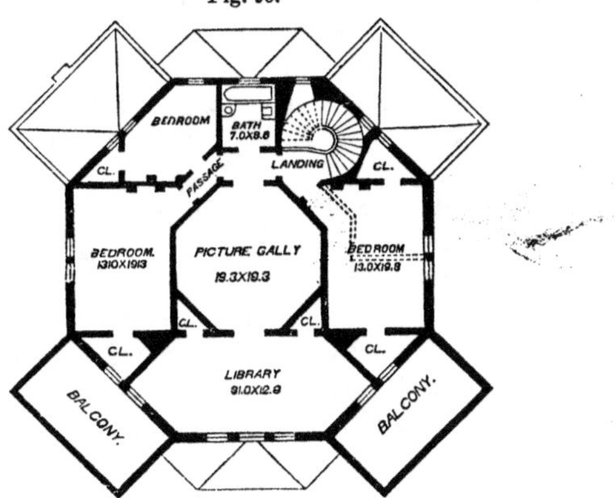

SECOND FLOOR PLAN.

side, a door opens into a symmetrical room in the form of an irregular hexagon. The extreme length of this room is 31.6 by 12.9 broad. These two rooms may be made to form, not only the most attractive feature of the house, but if skillfully treated will make a combination the like of which is rarely met with in a house of such limited extent as this. The octagon room may have a groined paneled ceiling, the ribs springing from Gothic columns attached to the walls at the angles of the room, and terminating against the angles of an octangular lantern-light surrounded by a richly ornamented cornice; the lantern to be filled in with stained glass, and to project a considerable height above the roof. The principal point of attraction in the adjoining room will be the noble Gothic window, which, if managed as a Gothic window may be managed, with mullions, cusps, foils, stained glass, and all the other etceteras, will, in conjunction with the octagon room, when the door is thrown open, have a magnificent effect.

Two balconies are provided in front; one over the conservatory, the other over the boudoir; to be entered from the front room.

The building has eight gables; it also has eight ridges and eight valleys, meeting at the lantern in the center. The gables are ornamented with verge boards of different patterns, so that each front presents a different appearance; and the chimneys are so contrived that the stacks will stand one half on each side of a ridge.

We give no estimate of the expense of this house, as it is one on which a great amount of ornamental work can be put to advantage, or it can be built quite plain. The style in which it is finished will, to a great degree, govern the expense. Plainly finished, it can be erected for $5,000; and $25,000 can be spent on it with ease, if the builder desires to make it what it can be made, one of the most unique and tasteful houses ever erected.

VIII.

BARNS, AND OTHER OUT-BUILDINGS.

There is the barn—and, as of yore,
I can smell the hay from the open door,
And see the busy swallows throng,
And hear the peewee's mournful song.
Oh, ye who daily cross the sill,
Step lightly, for I love it still;
And when you crowd the old barn eaves,
Then think what countless harvest sheaves
Have passed within that scented door,
To gladden eyes that are no more.—*T. B. Read.*

I.—PRELIMINARY REMARKS.

ALL that we need say in introduction to our designs may be embraced in a single paragraph. Let your out-buildings correspond in character with your house, and be as simple in plan and as unpretending in style as adaptation to their uses and an agreeable and appropriate external appearance will permit. A stable should pass for a stable, and not be so elaborate as to be mistaken for a farm-cottage. To build a poultry-house in the form of a palace is equally absurd. Let each seem to be just what it is, and present an example of complete fitness for the purpose of its erection.

Our designs, in general, require very little explanation, and speak for themselves. We present them in the hope that, where they may not be found exactly adapted to particular cases, they may, at least, furnish useful hints toward the thing required. Some of them have stood the test of actual construction and use, and have proved well adapted to their purposes.

II.—LEWIS F. ALLEN'S BARN.

We are indebted to the "Annual Register of Rural Afairs" for the accompanying design. It represents one of the best barns, probably, ever erected in this country, and, although much larger than will generally be required, furnishes a model in most respects for a structure of any desired size. We copy from the "Register" so much of the description as will serve our purpose:

"The body of the main barn is 100 feet long by 50 feet wide, the posts 18 feet high above the sill, making 9 bents. The beams are 14 feet above the sills, which is the height of the inner posts. The position of the floor and bays is readily understood from the plan. The floor, for a *grain* barn, is 14 feet wide, but may be contracted to 12 feet for one exclusively for hay. The area in front of the bays is occupied with a stationary horse-power and with machinery for various farm operations, such as threshing, shelling corn, cutting straw, crushing grain, etc., all of which is driven by bands from drums on the horizontal shaft overhead, which runs across the floor from the horse-power on the other side; this shaft being driven by a cog-wheel on the perpendicular shaft round which the horses travel.

"A passage four feet wide extends between the bays and the stables, which occupy the two wings. This extends up to the top of the bays, down which the hay is thrown for feeding, which renders this work as easy and convenient as possible.

"The floor of the main barn is three feet higher than that of the stables. This will allow a cellar under it, if desired—or a deeper extension of the bays—and it allows storage lofts over the cattle, with sufficient slope of roof. A short flight of steps at the ends of each passage admits easy access from the level of the barn floor.

"The line of mangers is two feet wide. A manure window is placed at every 12 feet. The stalls are double; that is, for two animals each, which are held to their places by a rope and chain, attached to a staple and ring at each corner of the stall. This mode is preferred to securing by stanchions. A pole or scantling, placed over their heads, prevents them from climbing so as to get their feet into the mangers, which they are otherwise very apt to do.

"The sheds, which extend on the three sides of the barn,

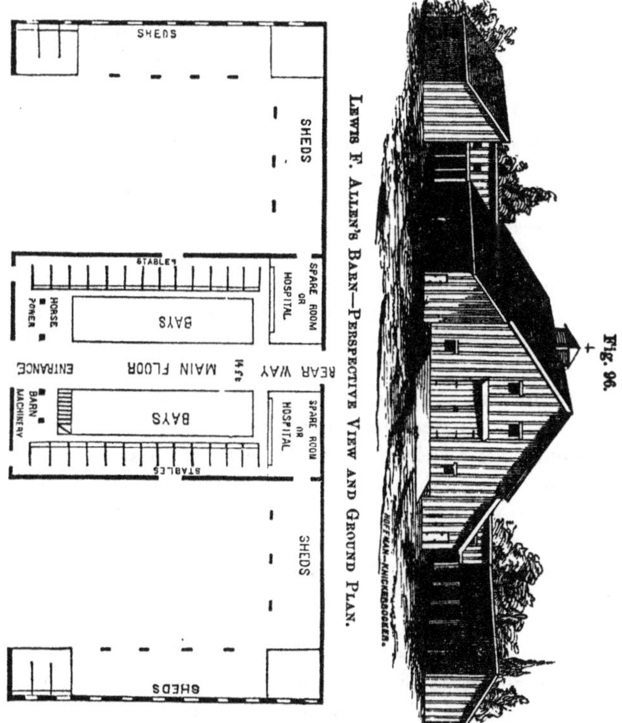

Fig. 96.

LEWIS F. ALLEN'S BARN—PERSPECTIVE VIEW AND GROUND PLAN.

and touch it at the rear end, are on a level with the stables. An *inclined plane*, from the main floor through the middle of the back shed, forms a rear egress for wagons and carts, descending three feet from the floor. The two rooms, one on each side of this rear passage, 16 by 34 feet, may be used for housing sick animals, cows about to calve, or any other purpose required. The stables at the front ends of the sheds are convenient for teams of horses or oxen, or they may be fitted for wagon-houses, tool-houses, or other purposes. The rooms, 16 feet square at the inner corners of the sheds, may be used for weak ewes, lambs, or for a bull-stable.

"Racks or mangers may be fitted up in the open sheds for feeding sheep or young cattle, and yards may be built adjoin ing, on the rear, six or eight in number, into which they may run and be kept separate. Barred partitions may separate the different flocks. Bars may also inclose the opening in front, or they may, if required, be boarded up tight. Step-ladders are placed at convenient intervals, for ascending the shed-lofts.

"A granary over the machine-room is entered by a flight of stairs. Poles extending from bay to bay, over the floor, will admit the storage of much additional hay or grain. As straw can not be well kept when exposed to the weather, and is at the same time becoming more valuable as its uses are better understood, we would suggest that the space on these cross poles be reserved for its deposit from the elevator from threshing grain, or until space is made for it in one of the bays.

"A one-sided roof is given to the sheds (instead of a double-sided), to throw all the water on the *outside*, in order to keep the interior of the yards dry. Eave-troughs take the water from the roofs to cisterns. The cisterns, if connected by an underground pipe, may be all drawn from by a single pump if necessary."

III.—MR. CHAMBERLAIN'S OCTAGON BARN.

The accompanying cut represents the ground plan of an octagon barn erected by Mr. Calvin Chamberlain, of Foxcroft, Maine, and described in the "Reports of the Board of Agriculture" of that State.

The plan is on a scale of 15 feet to the inch, which shows the structure to be a trifle over 36 feet in diameter.

"There is a cellar under the whole, eight feet deep, and a

cart-way leading out on a level. The floor is ten feet in the clear; doors same width and height; height below scaffold, seven and a half feet clear; entire height of walls, 19 feet. A door

Fig. 97.

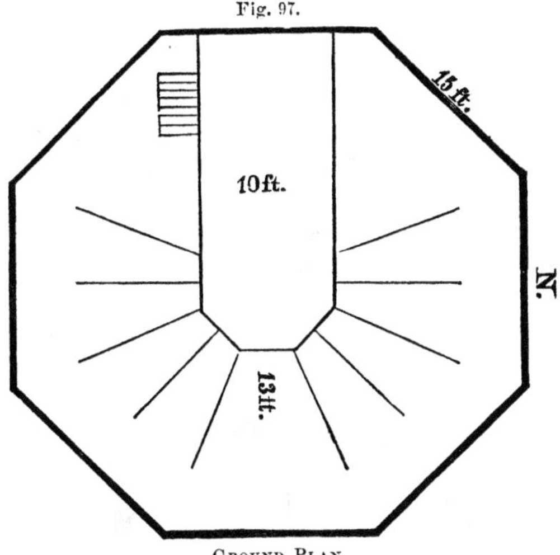

GROUND PLAN.

is shown opening north to the pasture, four feet wide and seven and a half feet high; one south, same size, opening to yard; one on southwest side communicates with other buildings. Stairs lead to cellar and hay-loft. Passage-way behind cattle stalls five feet wide, admitting wheelbarrow to pass at any time to any manure scuttle. Gates hanging to outer wall close passages to stalls, so that any animal may occupy its place untied. Side-lights at large doors, and a large window on opposite side, one sash of which slides horizontally, light the stable. Four large windows, set quite up to the plates, light the hay-loft. These let down at top, and are left down half the year; the two feet projection of the roof protects them from all storms. Cellar is lighted by four double windows and the side-light at head of stairs. The open space, 13 feet long, at end of floor, admits the horse, so that the hay-cart is brought to the center of the barn for unloading. A scaffold 13 feet long is put over the floor, and 12 feet above it."

This small barn, Mr. Chamberlain says, will store 20 tons of hay.

IV.—MR. BECKWITH'S OCTAGON BARN.

The annexed cut represents the basement plan of the barn erected by E. W. Beckwith, Principal of the Boys' Boarding School, at Cromwell, Middlesex County, Connecticut, in September, 1858.

The beauty and convenience of the arrangement for stalls and feeding can be seen at a glance. The octagon form is adopted because it is best adapted to inclose the desired plan.

This building, 30¼ feet short diameter, 12½ feet each side, or 100 feet inside circumference, and 13 feet each outside, or 104

Fig. 98.

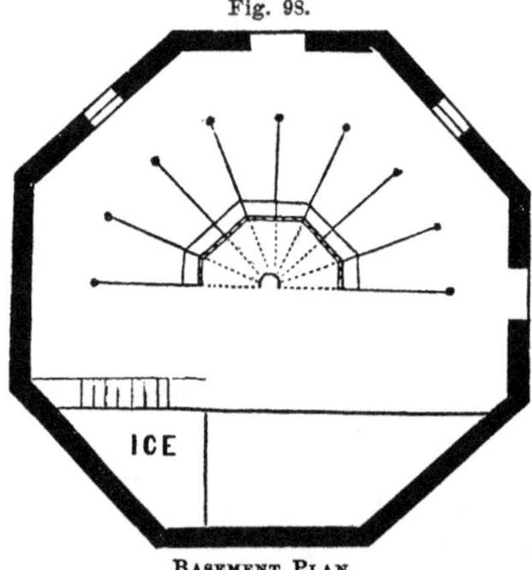

BASEMENT PLAN.

feet circumference when the wall is 14 inches thick, as in the present case, incloses an area of 750 feet.

The wall is grouted stone work, laid up between planks cut the right length for each inside and outside of angle, held to the proper distance apart by cast-iron clamps pierced with holes at each end to receive the iron dowels driven into each edge of the planks. These planks, when in an upright position on the wall, should be plumbed and staylathed preparatory to laying the stone. The basement floor is cemented, the horses standing on a movable slat-work, which keeps the bedding dry. The height of this story should be eight feet; the clear space from the stalls to the wall, four feet wide; the stalls six feet long, including manger-box, which leaves a circle in the center about ten feet diameter as the base of a cone, over which all the feed is thrown down to the animals. Under the cone is a fine place for a water-tank or pump.

The remaining space, when not wanted for stalls, furnishes room for cleaning off horses, for storing roots, for an ice-house, or any other purpose for which it may be wanted.

The feeding place is a hole about three feet square over the apex of the cone, which can be covered with a scuttle.

The walls are 26 feet high from the foundation, giving 16 feet altitude above the barn floor, which can be left clear and open to the roof, thus allowing the hay to be deposited in any direction and to any required proportion of the space; a gang-way to the feed-hole being left, or cut afterward, at option. There is one door, 9 by 10 feet, to this floor, for carriages, etc., the hay being taken in at a window on the up-hill side. Of course a place would be partitioned off if carriages are to be housed in the barn.

The cost of this stone barn, covered with mastic roofing at five cents a foot, will be about $325.

The walls cost $230, but closer personal attention would have made them cheaper. A wood barn on the same base-ment would have cost at least $40 more, and not be as good for many reasons.

There is nothing to burn by fire but one floor, and the roof and the walls would be left for another.

The utility of narrow stalls, in this case five feet wide at the broad end and two feet at the manger, may be questioned by some ; but you have that matter entirely according to fancy, the peculiar feature of this plan being that they all point to the center. It is peculiarly adapted to those gentlemen who wish to keep horses and cows, and be able to feed them without too much labor or time and exposure to dirt.

You can have a hired man or not, as you choose, which is sometimes desirable. This plan, if not adopted by others, may serve a good purpose as a suggester.

V.—A CIRCULAR BARN.

The barn, plans of which are herewith presented, was built by the Shakers of Berkshire County, Massachusetts, and is certainly worthy of the attention of farmers contemplating the

Fig. 99.

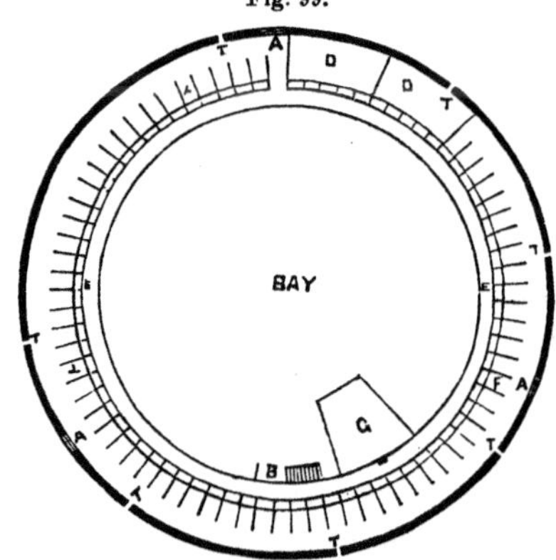

FIRST FLOOR PLAN.

A., doors ;* B., stairs ; D., calf-pens ; E., alleys ; F., stalls ; G., granary ; H., double doors ; T., windows.

erection of barns on a large scale. It is 100 feet diameter, built of stone—a material that is very abundant in that part of Massachusetts—two stories high, the first one being only seven and

* An error in the plans represents the doors as windows, and *vice versa*.

a half feet between floors, and contains stalls for seventy hea(of cattle, and two calf-stables. These stalls are situated in a circle next the outer wall, with the heads of the animals point-

Fig. 100.

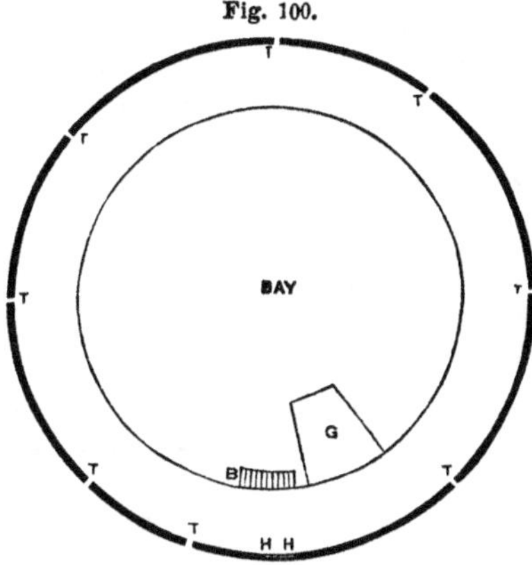

SECOND FLOOR PLAN.

ing inward, looking into an alley in which the feeder passes around in front of and looking into the face of every animal. The circle forming the stable and alley-way is 14 feet wide, inside of which is the great bay. Over the stable and alley is the threshing-floor, which is 14 feet wide and about 300 feet long on the outer side, into which a dozen loads of hay may be hauled, and all be unloaded at the same time into the bay in the center.

There should be a large chimney formed of timbers open in the center of such a mass of hay, connecting with air-tubes under the stable floor, extending out to the outside of the building, and with a large ventilator in the peak of the roof. We should also recommend an extension of the eaves beyond the outer wall, by means of brackets, so as to form a shed over the doors, and the manure thrown out of the stables and piled against the wall.

VI.—A SIDE-HILL BARN.

We copy the accompanying plans and the description from the *American Agriculturist* for September, 1858, where a perspective view of the barn is also given.

Entering the barn at either end, as shown in the main floor plan, there is a floor, either 12 or 14 feet wide, as may be most convenient, which passes through the entire length. On

Fig. 101.

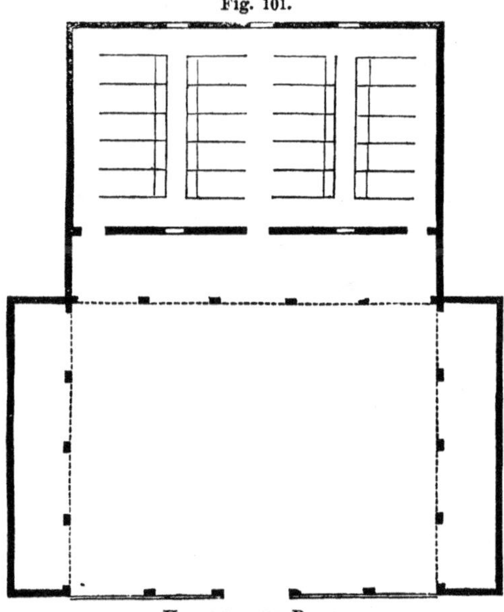

UNDERGROUND PLAN.

one side is a large bay for hay or grain in the sheaf. Opposite, in part, is another bay. Next to that a passage of five feet wide, to carry out straw or hay to throw down below into the yard. Next to the passage is a granary, and adjoining it a tool-house, or area for threshing machines, straw-cutters, etc., with a partition off from the floor, or not, at pleasure. Nine feet above the floor, on each side, should be a line of girts, connecting the inner posts, on which may be thrown loose poles to hold a temporary scaffold for the storage of hay, or grain in the sheaf, when required. By such arrangement the barn can be filled to the peak or ridge-pole, and the ventilator above will carry out all the heated air and moisture given off from the forage stored within. Slatted windows, or side ventilators, may be put in the side next to the yard, if required. The roof has a "third" pitch, or one foot rise to two feet in width, which lasts longer and gives more storage than a flatter one.

The frame of the barn above is 60 by 50 feet, with posts set upon stones below, to support the overshot sill, as shown in

Fig. 102.

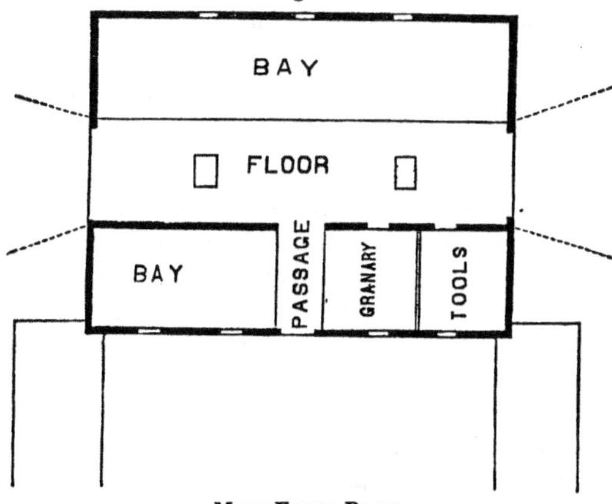

MAIN FLOOR PLAN.

the ground plan. Underneath are four lines of stalls, two on each side of the center passage-way, heading each other, with a four-foot feeding alley between them, receiving the forage from above, from which it is thrown into the mangers, two and a half feet wide, to which the cattle are tied or chained. The stalls are double, allowing two animals, if neat stock, in each. They are tied at the sides next the partitions, to prevent injury to each other. On the hill side are three windows in the upper part of the wall, to admit light and ventilation, either glazed or grated, as may be necessary.

The advantages of a side-hill barn are, the warmth of its stables in winter and their coolness in summer; storage for roots, if required; much additional room under the same roof, but not, we think, at diminished expense; and greater compactness of storage than in one on the common plan.

But it is essential to the comfort and convenience of the side-hill barn that it be well embanked with earth, so that the falling water may freely pass away from the walls; and that the stables and yards be well drained. Without these precautions, such barns are little better than nuisances, the rains and melting snows flooding everything beneath the building, and in the yards and sheds below.

There should be a flight of stairs (not represented in the plan) from the underground floor to that above.

SHELTER CHEAPER THAN FODDER.—An improvement on our present practice of shelter, and care of our animals, would be an equivalent to an actual shortening of winter. It can hardly be questioned that exposure of cattle to extreme cold injures their health, and thus interferes with the owner's profit. Chemical physiology teaches us that warmth is equivalent to a certain portion of food, and that an animal exposed to more cold will eat more, and one better housed and warmer kept will eat less. To keep an animal comfortable, therefore, is to save food; and this alone is a sufficient inducement to provide that comfort to the full extent.*—*Maine Agricultural Report.*

——Every animal should have its own particular stall in the stable, and should be allowed in no other.

---

* It is asserted, on good authority, that exposed animals will consume a third more food, and come out in the spring in worse condition.

VII.—STABLES.*

The subject of stables—their construction, arrangement of accommodations, etc.—is one to which a volume might profitably be devoted; but our present object is merely to furnish a

Fig. 103. Fig. 104.

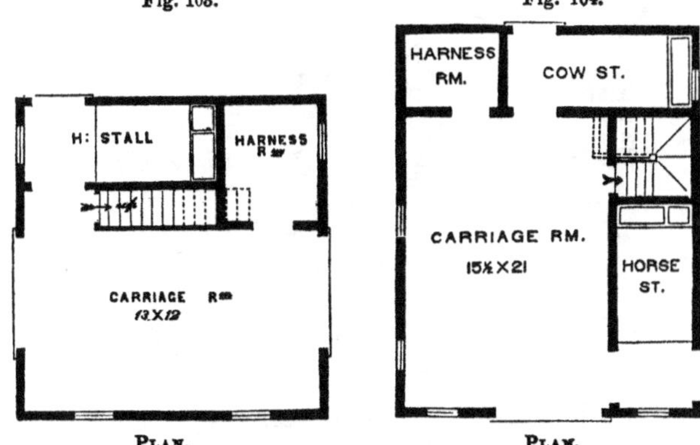

PLAN. PLAN.

few designs adapted to execution in connection with country houses and villas, and to show how they may be planned, as

Fig. 105.

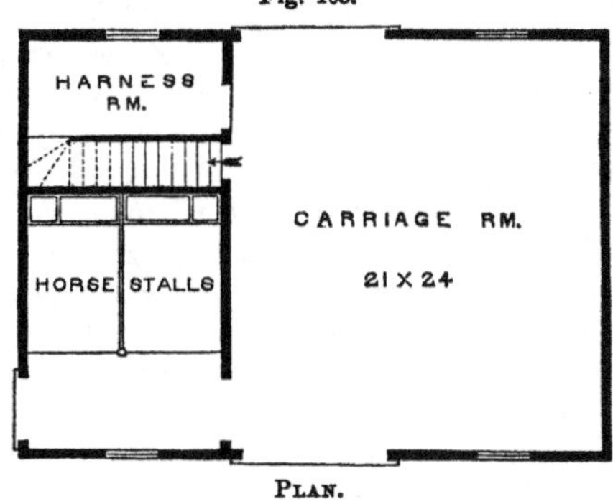

PLAN.

* F. E. Graef, Architect, 56 Wall Street, New York.

in fig. 103, for one horse and carriage; in fig. 104, for one horse and two vehicles; or, as in fig. 105, with which we give an elevation (fig. 106), for two horses and three vehicles.

Fig. 106.

FRONT ELEVATION.

Constructed of wood in a proper manner, fig. 103 will cost $125; fig. 104, $185; and fig. 105, $275. Built of brick, they will generally cost a little over a third more.

ELEVATORS IN BARNS.—In large barns the pitching up of the hay into the upper part of the bays is a very laborious process and requires considerable time. In such cases an *elevator*, like that of the best threshing machine, to be worked by the two horses removed from the loaded wagon of hay, may be profitably employed, greatly lessening the labor and quickening the operation. The same elevator would be used in carrying threshed straw from the machine to the bays. The simplest and best elevator for this purpose is made of a light, inclined board platform, four feet wide, on each side of which a rope or endless chain runs, connected by cross-bars, a foot or two apart, which slide over the upper surface of this platform, and sweep the hay upward as fast as pitched upon it.

VIII.—AN OCTAGON POULTRY HOUSE.

This design is selected from Bement's "Poulterer's Companion." It has been executed, we believe, near Factoryville, Staten Island. It is ten feet in diameter and six feet and a half high. The sills are 4 by 4, and the plates 3 by 4 joists, halved and nailed at the joints. It is sided with inch and a quarter spruce plank, tongued and grooved. No upright timbers are used. The floor and roofing are of the same kind of

Fig. 107.

PERSPECTIVE VIEW.

plank. To guard against leakage by shrinking, the joints may be battened with lath or strips of thin boards. An eight-square frame supports the top of the rafters, leaving an opening of ten inches in diameter, on which is placed an octagon chimney for a ventilator, which makes a very pretty finish. The piers should be either cedar, chestnut, or locust, two feet high, and set on flat stones.

The letter D designates the door; W, W, windows; L, latticed window to admit air, with a shutter to exclude it, when necessary; E, entrance for the fowls, with a sliding door; P, platform for the fowls to alight on when going in; R, R, roosts placed spirally, one end attached to a post near the center of the room, and the other end to the wall; the first, or lowermost one, two feet from the floor, and the others 18 inches apart, and rising gradually to the top, six feet from the floor. These roosts will accommodate 40 ordinary-sized fowls. F, F, is a board floor, on an angle of about 45 degrees, to catch and carry down the droppings of the fowls. This arrangement renders it much more convenient in cleaning out the manure, which should be frequently done.

Fig. 108.

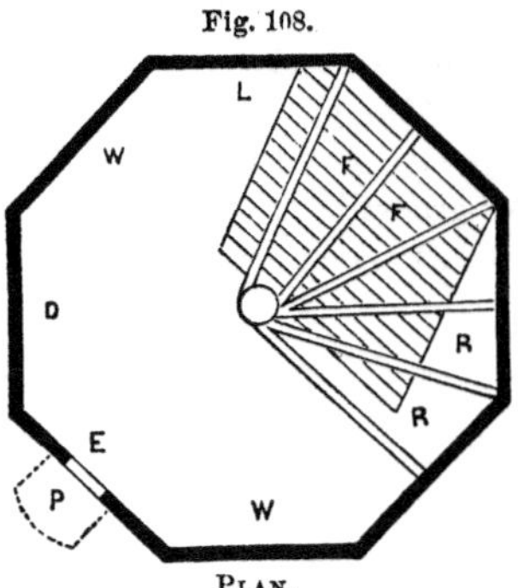

PLAN.

The space beneath this floor is appropriated to nests, 12 in number, 15 inches wide, 18 inches deep, and 18 inches high. In order to give an appearance of secrecy, which it is well known the hen is so partial to, the front is latticed with strips of lath. By this arrangement a free circulation of air is admitted, which adds much to the comfort of the hens while sitting.

The object of placing this house on piles is to prevent the encroachments of rats, mice, skunks, etc., and is a good method, as rats are very annoying, especially where they have a good harbor under the house, often destroying the eggs and killing the young chickens.

TWO ERRORS.—It is an error to build a house upon a side-hill with an "underground kitchen;" but it is a greater error to build a barn without such a room upon the down-hill side, and if possible having a southern exposure. In this room all the horned cattle should be stabled, having a yard to themselves entirely separate from any other stock. The horse stable should always be on the ground floor, with an entrance from a separate yard.

IX.—AN OCTAGON PIGGERY.

The accompanying design shows the plan of an economically constructed and convenient piggery. It may, of course, be enlarged to any desired extent without any change of form or

Fig. 109.

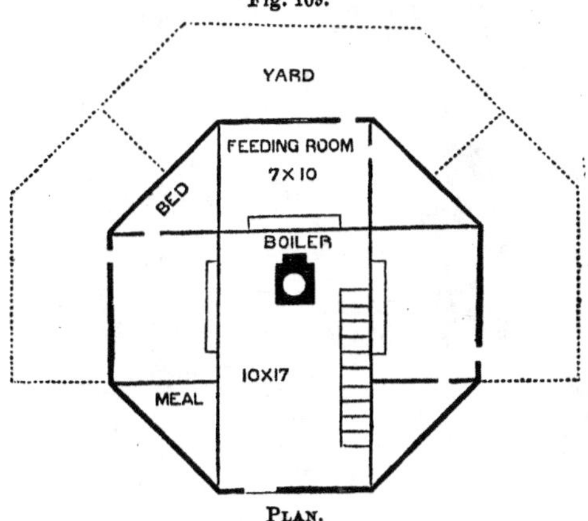

PLAN.

arrangement. The elevation may be similar to that of the poultry-house (fig. 107), and should have sufficient height to furnish a good upper room for storing corn, etc., for the swine.

X.—AN ASHERY AND SMOKE-HOUSE.

An ashery and smoke-house combined may be economically built as represented in our design. The first story, or ash-pit, should be built of stone or hard brick, and be provided with an iron door. The walls need not be more than from six to eight feet in height. The ceiling should be lathed and plastered.

The smoke-house story above may be of wood. It is entered in the rear on a level with the ground. Four tin tubes, introduced through the floor, admit the smoke from the ash-room below, where the fire is kindled. This arrangement precludes all danger from fire, secures the meat against being overheated

Fig. 110.

AN ASHERY AND SMOKE-HOUSE.

in smoking, and gives a clean and convenient smoke-room. It may be ventilated either through the gable or the roof.

A side-hill situation is by no means essential in this mode of construction. Both stories may be above ground, the smoke-house door being reached by outside stairs or a step-ladder.

XI.—AN ICE-HOUSE.

The first grand essential in the construction of an ice-house is the perfect inclosure of the space to be occupied by the ice with walls and floors which shall prove non-conductors of

Fig. 111.

A CIRCULAR ICE-HOUSE—PERSPECTIVE VIEW.

heat. The second important point is to secure perfect drainage. These conditions attained, the rest is comparatively unimportant.

A common and entirely effective mode of constructing an ice-house is thus described:

The frame or sides should be formed of two ranges of upright joists about six by four inches; the lower ends to be put in the ground without any sill; the upper to be morticed into the timbers which are to support the upper floor. The joists in the two ranges should be each opposite another. They should then be lined or faced with rough boarding, which need not be very tight. These boards should be nailed to those edges of the joists nearest each other, so that one range of joists shall be outside the building and the other inside the ice-room, as shown in fig. 112. Cut out or leave out a space for a door of suitable dimensions on the north or west side, higher than the ice will come, and board up the inner side of this opening so as to form a door-casing on each side. Two doors should be attached to this opening—one on the inner side and one on the outward, both opening outward. The space between these partitions should be filled with charcoal-dust, tan, or saw-dust, whichever can be the most readily obtained.

Fig. 112.

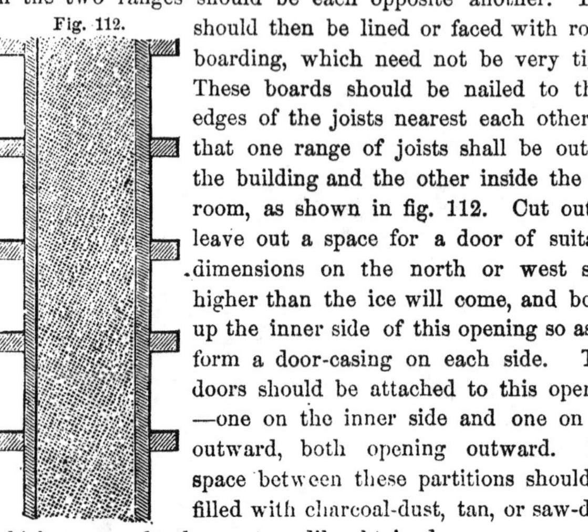

The bottom of the ice vault should be filled about a foot deep with small blocks of wood or round stones; these are leveled and covered with wood-shavings, over which a plank floor to receive the ice should be laid; some spread straw a foot thick over the floor, and lay the ice on that. A floor should also be laid on the beams above the vault, on which place several inches of tan or saw-dust. The roof should be perfectly tight, and it is usually best to give it a considerable pitch. The space between the roof and the flooring beneath should be ventilated by means of a door or lattice window in each gable. The drain can be constructed in accordance with the situation, the only things requiring attention being to have it carry off all the water settling at the bottom, and not be so open as to allow the passage of air into the vault.

Fig. 113 represents a section of such an ice-house. We give a perspective view of a circular ice-house, which is constructed on the same principle. It may advantageously be executed in

Fig. 113.

concrete. Ventilation is secured by leaving a small aperture in the peak of the roof, protected by a hood or cap, as shown.

Should an underground house be preferred, the plan of building can be the same; or a less expensive method may be used. A side-hill having a northern exposure affords a desirable location. In such case one end of the house is usually above ground. The boards can be of the cheapest description, and the space or air-chamber filled in with straw; the ground forming the support to the whole. No less attention should be paid to draining than in the other case; and when in use, the space between the ice and the peak of the roof should be filled with straw.

XII.—AN APIARY.

Fig. 114 represents a design for a rustic apiary or bee-house, which strikes us as being far more beautiful and appropriate than the elaborately ornamented temple or palace-like structures we sometimes see. The mode of its construction is readily

Fig. 114.

PERSPECTIVE VIEW.

seen. It may, of course, be made of any desirable size on the same plan. [For directions in reference to the construction of hives, the best site for an apiary, and instructions in bee-keeping, see "Domestic Animals."*]

*** Domestic Animals: a Pocket Manual of Horse, Cattle, and Sheep Husbandry; or, How to Breed, Rear, and Use all the Common Domestic Animals. Embracing Descriptions of the various Breeds of Horses, Cattle, Sheep, Swine, Poultry, etc.; the "Points" or Characteristics by which to judge Animals; Feeding and General Management of Stock; How to Improve Breeds; How to Cure Sick Animals, etc. With a Chapter on Bees. Handsomely illustrated. Price, in paper, 30 cents; in muslin, 50 cents. Fowler and Wells, Publishers.**

How many expensive, not to say fatal, errors in the buying, selling, breeding, and management of farm-stock might be avoided by means of the practical information and plain common sense advice condensed into this comprehensive and thorough little Hand-book!

XIII.—A PLAY-HOUSE.

Build your children a play-house of some sort. A very rude affair will please them, but something similar to the ac-

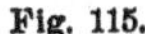

Fig. 115.

PERSPECTIVE VIEW.

companying design will please you too, and be a highly ornamental feature in your grounds. The construction is simple, but the effect is very fine.

MATERIALS FOR RUSTIC STRUCTURES.—In order to succeed in constructing rustic work, the first thing is to procure *the materials.* All such objects as may be exposed to the weather should be of the most durable wood, of which red cedar is best. For certain purposes, white oak will answer well, but as it is essential to have the bark remain on, the wood should be cut at a time of year when this will not peel or separate. If cut toward the close of summer, the wood will last about twice as long as when cut in winter or spring. A horse-load or two, of boughs or branches of trees, of which a goodly portion may be curved and twisted, from one to six inches in diameter, will constitute the materials for a good beginning.—*J. J. Thomas.*

XIV.—A RUSTIC GARDEN HOUSE.

A rustic structure, like the one here represented, when covered with vines and climbing shrubs, forms one of the most

Fig. 116.

PERSPECTIVE VIEW.

beautiful and appropriate objects that a lawn or flower garden can boast. Furnished with rustic seats, it becomes an attractive summer resort in which to work or read.

IX.

THE CHURCH AND THE SCHOOL-HOUSE.

On other shores, above their moldering towns,
In sullen pomp the tall cathedral frowns—
Pride in its aisles and paupers at the door,
Which feeds the beggars which it fleeced of yore
Simple and frail, our lowly temples throw
Their slender shadows on the paths below.—*Holmes.*

In a green lane that from the village street
Diverges, stands the school-house.—*Street.*

I.—A VILLAGE CHURCH.*

HE accompanying design (figs. 117, 118, 119) represents a country church, and, as has been more or less the case with all our designs, is intended to show how easy it is, without costly materials, and without expensive details, but with due regard to proportion, symmetry, and harmony of style, to produce a structure at once pleasing, chaste, and adapted to its purposes. The piles of brick work and the wooden boxes which so often pass for churches among us, but are, to say the least, a reproach to our cultivated society, bear witness, on every hand, to the frequency with which the first principles of architecture are

---

* F. E. Graef, Architect, 56 Wall Street, New York.

Fig. 117.—A Village Church—Perspective View.

sinned against through ignorance. It is this ignorance that we hope to aid in dissipating, both by precept and example.

The height of this church from the floor to the eaves is 17 feet, and the whole height of the ceiling about 22 feet. It is planned for a gallery across the front merely. It will seat 400 people. The same ground plan may of course be so executed as to give considerably greater accommodations. By making the ceiling higher, for instance, side galleries may be introduced. If required, a lecture-room and Sunday-schoolroom may be added on the rear; but if the location be suitable, these accommodations may be secured at less cost in a basement.

Fig. 118.

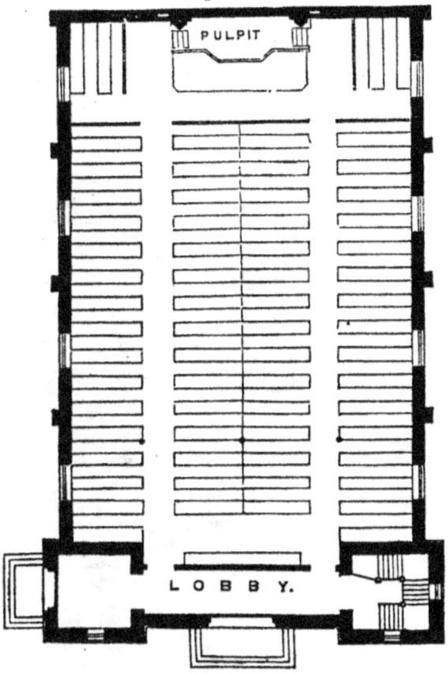

GROUND FLOOR PLAN.

The walls are to be built of brick, the exterior projections being faced with front brick, costing about $10 per thousand. The window sills, door sills, caps, and steps are to be of cut stone. The roof, cornices, and cupola are to be of wood. The main roof is to be covered with slate, and the tower roof and cupola to be tinned. Finished inside in a liberal manner the cost is estimated at about $9,800; or finished quite plainly, it can be built for less than $9,000.

Fig. 119.

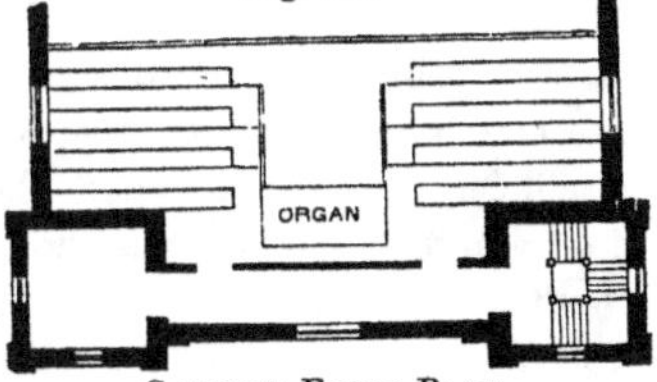

GALLERY FLOOR PLAN.

II.—A VILLAGE SCHOOL-HOUSE.*

This design represents a single two-story school-house suitable for a small village or other country place. The first and second stories are almost entirely alike in their arrangements. Each room will accommodate fifty-two pupils, and has recitation benches in front of the teacher's desk. The easy ingress and egress afforded by the broad halls and stairs; the large sep-

Fig. 120.

FRONT ELEVATION.

arate wardrobes for the two sexes; the convenient position of the teacher's desk with its large wall-space for the blackboard, are sufficiently apparent upon the plan. A recitation-room and a room for apparatus may be added on the rear, if desired, without changing the rest of the plan.

The walls are of brick, eight inches thick, strengthened by pilasters (4×20 inches), which serve both for use and orna-

* F. E. Graef, Architect, 56 Wall Street, New York.

ment, as may be seen by examining the plan and elevations. The inside of the walls is furred off as usual. The front part, under the hall and clothes-closets, is intended to be dug out for a coal and furnace cellar. A portable furnace, costing from $75 to $100, will heat the whole house, and is to be preferred to stoves. In addition to the opposite windows, which facilitate ventilation during the warm season, ventilating shafts,

Fig. 121.

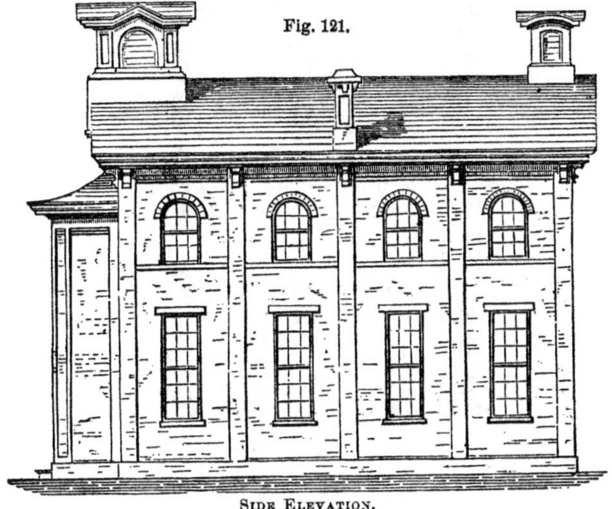

SIDE ELEVATION.

terminating in a box on the roof, are indicated in the rear wall. The inside walls are to have two coats of plaster, and be wainscoted up to the windows all around. The roof may be covered with slate or shingles, as most convenient. The bell cupola, very appropriately a prominent ornamental and useful feature in school architecture, may be constructed of wood, as shown. Access to it may be had from the second floor hall, by means of a step-ladder. The school-room furniture consists of double desks, about three and a half feet long, with stools.

All school-houses should, if possible, be constructed of solid materials—brick or stone—in so substantial a manner as to outlast all the other buildings in the town or village, and serve for the accommodation of many generations of children, whose

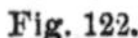

Fig. 122.

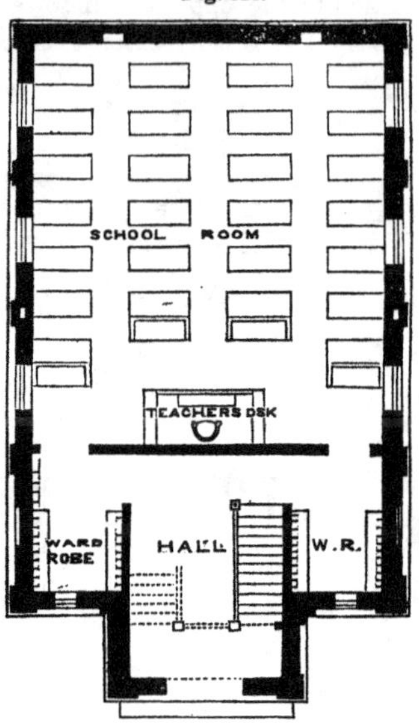

PLAN.

prominent destructiveness they are better calculated to resist than any wooden building can be.

The estimated cost of this school-house is within $1,700.

APPENDIX.

A.

HOW TO BUILD WITH ROUGH STONE.

Let the quarrymen split it off just as the veins of the stone make it most easily worked. Select such pieces as, from their length and even quality, seem adapted for sills and lintels, and use the remainder just in the shape it naturally comes upon your ground from the quarry. In building your walls, lay the stone in its exact bed as it lay in the quarry, and here and there let long pieces be introduced, the length of the thickness of your walls; these, lying across, would serve as *bonders* to the walls, and will materially strengthen the work. A wall built in this manner, in irregular courses, looks remarkably well for country buildings, and it is the method in which the time-honored rural churches of England have been built, than which more simply beautiful or more durable erections can not be found.—Gervase Wheeler.

B.

HOLLOW BRICK WALLS.

Fig. 123.

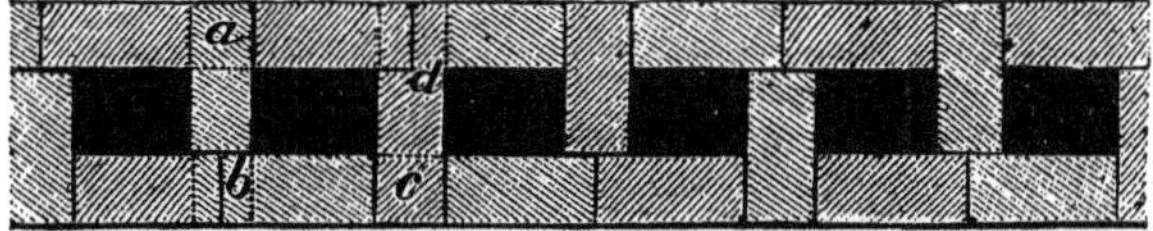

Simple Mode of Building a Hollow Wall.

Fig. 123. shows a very simple and cheap mode of building a hollow wall twelve inches wide, which answers very well for low additions, or walls intended to bear but little weight. An addition of another brick to the outside would make a good sixteen-inch wall. The tie-bricks alternate in the courses; that is, the brick *a* is covered in the next course with the brick *b* (shown by the *dotted* lines); *c* by *d*, and so on through the whole.—Downing.

C.

UNBURNT BRICK FOR BUILDING.

The following particulars are compiled from the Report made by Mr. Ellsworth while Commissioner of Patents:

Almost every kind of clay will answer; it is tempered by treading it with cattle, and cut straw is added, at the rate of two bundles of straw to clay enough for one hundred bricks. It is then ready for molding. It is found that the most economical size for the bricks for building such cottages is the following, viz., one foot long, six inches wide, and four inches thick.

The cellar or foundation must be formed of stone or burnt brick.

In damp soils, the dampness should be prevented from rising from the soil into the unburnt wall by laying one course of slate, or of brick, laid in cement or hydraulic mortar, at the top of the foundation.

The walls of the cottage are laid up one foot in thickness of the unburnt brick. This thickness is exactly the length of the brick, or the width of two bricks, and the strongest wall is made by laying the work with alternate courses of *leaders* and *stretchers* (*i. e.*, one course with the bricks laid across the wall, the next course side by side). A weak mortar of lime and sand is generally used for laying the bricks, but a good brick mortar is preferable. Where lime is scarce, a mortar composed of three parts clay, one part sand, and two parts wood-ashes, answers very well as a substitute for lime mortar. The division walls may be six inches thick, just the width of the brick; but when the cottage has rooms wider than twelve feet, it is better to make the first-story partitions two bricks thick. The doors and window frames being ready to insert, the cottage is very rapidly built. These frames are made of stout plank, of the exact thickness of the walls, so that the casing inside and outside helps to strengthen the wall and covers the joints. If lintels and sills of stone are not to be had, pieces of timber three inches thick, of the same width as the wall, and a foot longer on each side than the opening, may be used instead.

The roof may be of shingles or thatch, and it is indispensable in a cottage of unburnt clay that it should project two feet all around, so as completely to guard the walls from vertical rains. The *outside* of the wall is plastered with good lime mortar mixed with hair, and then with a second coat, pebble-dashed, as in *rough-cast* walls. The inside of the wall is plastered and whitewashed in the common way.

Built in the simple way of the prairies, these cottages are erected for an incredibly small sum, costing no more than log houses, while they are far more durable and agreeable in appearance.

But we have also seen highly ornamental cottages built of this material, the bricks made entirely by the hands of the owner or occupant, and the whole erected at a cost of not more than one half of that paid for the same cottage built in an equally comfortable manner of wood or brick. When plastered or rough-cast on the exterior, this mode of construction presents to the eye the same effect as an ordinary stuccoed house, while it is warmer and far less costly in repairs than any other cheap material is.

D.

DR. BUCHANAN ON CELLARS.

While I would condemn cellars and basements entirely, the common plan of building in their absence must be condemned also. The house being built above the surface of the earth, a space is left between the lower floor and the ground, which is even closer and darker than a cellar, and which becomes, on a smaller scale, the source of noxious emanations. Under-floor space should be abolished as well as cellars and basements. The plan that I have adopted with the most satisfactory success, to avoid all these evils, is the following: Let the house be built entirely above the ground; let the lower floor be built upon the surface of the earth, at least as high as the surrounding soil. If filled up with any clean material a few inches above the surrounding earth, it would be better. A proper foundation being prepared, make your first floor by a pavement of brick, laid in hydraulic cement upon the surface of the ground. Let the same be extended into your walls, so as to cut off the walls of your house with water-proof cement from all communication with the moisture of the surrounding earth. Upon this foundation build according to your fancy. Your lower floor will be perfectly dry—impenetrable to moisture and to vermin; not a single animal can get a lodgment in your lower story. By adopting this plan, your house will be dry and cleanly; the atmosphere of your ground-floor will be fresh and pure; you will be entirely relieved from that steady drain upon life which is produced by basements and cellars; and if you appropriate the ground-floor to purposes of store-rooms, kitchen, etc., you will find that the dry apartments thus constructed are infinitely superior to the old basements and cellars. And if you place your sitting and sleeping rooms on the second and third floors, you will be as thoroughly exempt from local miasma as architecture can make you.—DR. BUCHANAN.

E.

RECIPES FOR PAINTS, WASHES, STUCCO, ETC.

1. *Paints for Outside Work.*—The following recipes for mixing several desirable colors are from Wheeler's " Homes for the People :"

1. A cool gray, similar to what would be the tint of unpainted timber after a few years, may be obtained as follows:

Indian red, half a pound;
Lampblack, three ounces;
Raw umber, half a pound
White lead, one hundred pounds.

This color will be changed by the addition of sand, which in all cases is recommended, in a proportion of about one quart to every one hundred pounds of mixed color. The finest and whitest sand that the neighborhood affords should be used, and as its hue differs, so will the tint of the paint be changed.

This color, with one third less white, is very suitable for roofs, and is a cool, unreflecting gray tint of great softness and beauty.

2. A soft, pleasant tint, like that of coffee greatly diluted with milk, is oftentimes well adapted to a building, particularly in regions where red sandstone or other similar objects, with such local coloring, give a brown hue to portions of the landscape.

It may be mixed as follows:

Yellow ochre, five pounds;
Burnt umber, half a pound;
Indian red, quarter of a pound;
Chrome yellow, No. 1, half a pound, with one hundred pounds of white lead.

The key-notes in this color are the Indian red and the chrome yellow, and the tone may be brightened or lowered by more or less of either, as individual taste may prefer.

3. A still more delicate tint, resembling the pure color of the Caen stone, and well adapted for a large building with many beaks of outlines, may be mixed thus:

Yellow ochre, two pounds;
Vandyke brown, quarter of a pound;
Indian red, quarter of a pound;
Chrome yellow, No. 1, half a pound to every one hundred pounds of lead.

The following cheap and excellent paint for cottages is recommended by Downing. It forms a hard surface, and is far more durable than common paint. It will be found preferable to common paint for picturesque country houses of all kinds.

Take freshly-burned unslaked lime and reduce it to powder. To one peck or one bushel of this add the same quantity of fine white sand or fine coal ashes, and twice as much fresh wood ashes, all these being sifted through a fine sieve. They should then be thoroughly mixed together while dry. Afterward mix them with as much common linseed oil as will make the whole thin enough to work freely with a painter's brush.

This will make a paint of a light gray stone color, nearly white.

To make it fawn or drab, add yellow ochre and Indian red; if drab is desired, add burnt umber, Indian red, and a little black; if dark stone color, add lampblack; or if brown stone, then add Spanish brown. All these colors should of course be first mixed in oil and then added.

This paint is very much cheaper than common oil paint. It is equally well suited to wood, brick, or stone. It is better to apply it in two coats; the first thin, the second thick.

2. *A Cheap Wash.*—For the outside of wooden cottages, barns, out-buildings, fences, etc., where economy must be consulted, the following wash is recommended:

Take a clean barrel that will hold water. Put into it half a bushel of quicklime, and slake it by pouring over it boiling water sufficient to cover it four or five inches deep, and stirring it until slaked. When quite slaked dissolve it in water, and add two pounds of sulphate of zinc and one of common salt, which may be had at any of the druggists, and which in a few days will cause the whitewash to harden on the woodwork. Add sufficient water to bring it to the consistency of thick whitewash.

To make the above wash of a pleasant cream color, add three pounds of yellow ochre.

For fawn color, add four pounds of umber, one pound of Indian red, and one pound of lampblack.

For gray or stone color, add four pounds of raw umber and two pounds of lampblack.

The color may be put on with a common whitewash brush, and will be found much more durable than common whitewash.—*Horticulturist.*

For a wash for barns the *Horticulturist* also gives this:

Hydraulic cement, one peck; freshly slaked lime, one peck; yellow ochre (in powder), four pounds; burnt umber, four pounds; the whole to be "dissolved" in hot water, and applied with a brush.

3. *Staining Interior Wood Work.*—One of the simplest and best modes of staining pine or other soft wood is the following as given by Downing:

First prepare the wood by washing it with a solution of sulphuric acid, made by mixing it in the proportion of one ounce of sulphuric acid to a pint of warm water. It should be mixed when wanted and put on while warm, washing it evenly over every part to be stained.

Second, stain the wood so prepared by rubbing it lightly with tobacco stain, using a piece of flannel or sponge for this purpose. By merely coating it evenly in this way the natural grain of the wood will assume a dark tone, so as to resemble black walnut or oak; the effect of certain parts may be heightened by a little skill in mottling or slightly graining the wood, by repeating the coat and allowing it to settle in places.

When the stained wood is entirely dry, brush it over, in order to preserve it, with the following mixture: half a pound of beeswax, half a pint of linseed oil, and one pint of boiled linseed oil.

It may, if desired, afterward be varnished and polished. To make the above tobacco stain, take six pounds of common shag or "negro head" tobacco; boil it in as many quarts of water as will cover the tobacco, letting it simmer away slowly till it is of the consistence of syrup. Strain it, and it is ready for use.

We may add, that when it is desired to give the wood the tone of light oak or maple, the solution of sulphuric acid should be much weaker, and only a light coat of the stain should be used. Where a dark tone is preferred, two coats of the stain should be put on.

4. *Stucco and Stuccoing.*—Take stone lime fresh from the kiln and of the *best quality*, such as is known to make a strong and durable mortar (like the Thomaston lime). Slake it by sprinkling or pouring over it just water enough

to leave it when slaked in the condition of a fine *dry powder*, and not a *paste*. Set up a quarter-inch wire screen at an inclined plane, and throw this powder against it. What passes through is fit for use. That which remains behind contains the *core*, which would spoil the stucco, and must be rejected.

Having obtained the sharpest sand to be had, and having washed it, so that not a particle of the mud and dirt (which destroy the tenacity of most stuccoes) remains, and screened it to give some uniformity to the size, mix it with the lime in powder, in the proportion of *two parts sand* to one part lime. This is the best proportion for lime stucco. More lime would make a stronger stucco, but one by no means so hard—and hardness and tenacity are both needed.

The mortar must now be made by adding water, and working it thoroughly. On the *tempering* of the mortar greatly depends its tenacity.

The wall to be stuccoed should be first prepared by clearing off all loose dirt, mortar, etc., with a stiff broom. Then apply the mortar in two coats; the first a rough coat, to cover the inequalities of the wall, the second as a finishing coat. The latter, however, should be put on *before* the former is dry, and as soon, indeed, as the first coat is sufficiently firm to receive it; the whole should then be well floated, troweled, and marked off; and if it is to be colored in water-color, the wash should be applied, so as to *set* with the stucco.—DOWNING.

5. *Rough-Cast.*—The mode of putting on rough-cast is as follows:

The surface of the wall being brushed off clean, lay on a coat of good lime and hair mortar. Allow this to dry, and then lay on another coat as evenly and smoothly as possible without floating. As soon as two or three yards of the second coat is finished, have ready a pail of *rough-cast*, and splash or throw it on the wall. This is usually done by another workman, who holds the trowel with which he throws on the rough-cast in one hand, and a whitewash brush dipped constantly in the pail in the other, which follows the trowel until the whole is smooth and evenly colored.

The rough-cast itself is made of sharp sand, washed clean, screened, and mixed in a large tub with pure, newly slaked lime and water, till the whole is in a semi-fluid state. A little yellow ochre mixed in the rough-cast gives the whole a slighly fawn-colored shade, more agreeable to the eye than white.—DOWNING.

F.

ROOFING.

The following brief essay on roofing has been kindly furnished by a practical builder, Mr. Richardson, who has had extensive experience in this special department, in various parts of the United States. His hints are valuable.

The most important point to be observed in order to have a tight roof is, to use well-seasoned sheathing. If it is tongued and grooved, so much the better. Have it well nailed. The best material to cover your roof with is slate, if it is a steep roof. In the northern section of the United States and the Canadas, it is well to put a layer of felt on the sheathing before slating, as it will prevent the snow in winter and the rain in summer from driving under the slates. In the Middle States metallic roofing stands well; but in the extreme South and North, the expansion and contraction are so great, that it is almost impossible to have a tight roof, and it is only by giving them a coat of paint every other year that they answer at all. Copper, zinc, galvanized iron, and tin are the metals required for roofing purposes. Within a year or two, corrugated galvanized iron has been introduced on many of the government buildings, and has generally proved satisfactory. Its great cost will, however, exclude its extensive use among private buildings, as slate is better and costs less. One of the many improvements in the construction of buildings, at the present day, is the adaptation of the flat roof in place of the old-fashioned pitch roof. The many advantages gained in the number of better ventilated rooms, instead of the little, hot chambers of the old style, are so obvious, that no other argument would seem to be necessary to insure its universal adaptation, to say nothing of its great advantage in case of fire in the immediate neighborhood, or its use in a crowded city.

Perhaps one word in regard to the many different "patent roofing" materials now before the public may be of service. We have paid some attention to the merit claimed for each, and can safely recommend one, and that is "Warren's Improved Fire and Water Proof Roofing." This article has stood the test of time, and is considered by many of the best architects and builders a better article for flat roofing than any metal. All insurance companies insure buildings covered with this roofing at the same rate as slate.

We have recently had an opportunity to examine some extensive warehouses in New Orleans, which have been covered with the roofing some five years, and it is apparently as good as the day it was put on. The fact that it has been extensively used in the North and the Canadas, for many years, adds greatly to our confidence in its intrinsic value. Recollect this fact—you can never have a tight roof, no matter what you cover it with, unless you use well-seasoned sheathing boards, and have them well nailed.

G.

HOW TO BUILD CONCRETE HOUSES.

The following excellent practical directions are from the pen of Mr. D. Redmond, of Georgia, editor of the *Southern Cultivator*, and appeared originally in *Life Illustrated:*

1. *Location, etc.*—Select, if possible, a dry situation, and get all heavy materials, such as rock, sand, lime, gravel, etc., on the spot as early in the season as possible, say by the first or middle of May, in order that you may avail yourself of the long, warm days of summer for successfully carrying on your operations.

2. *Materials.*—The proper *materials* are *lime*, *sand*, coarse and fine *gravel*, large and small *rock*, and *water*. The lime may be from any good, pure limestone that will slack readily, and "*set*" or harden thoroughly when dry;* the sand

* The lime used by us is of a peculiar quality, known here as "hydraulic

should be sharp, and as free from clay, loam, and other earthy matter as possible; and the gravel and rock may be of any size, from that of a boy's marble up to eighteen inches or two feet square, according to the thickness of your walls.

3. *Foundation.*—Having fixed on your plan, lay off the *foundation*, and dig a trench two feet wide and two feet deep, the area or full size of your outer wall. With a heavy piece of hard wood, squared or rounded at the lower end, pound or ram down the earth in the bottom of this trench, going over it repeatedly, until it is solid and compact. A layer of hydraulic cement mortar, two inches thick, spread evenly over the bottom of the trenches thus compacted, gives you a solid foundation to start on, as soon as it "*sets*" or becomes hard. If you intend carrying up inside division walls of concrete, the foundation for these should be laid in the same way. Good hydraulic cement will take at least three parts of sharp sand; but it must be used as soon as mixed, or it will "*set*" and become useless.

4. *Frame and Boxing.*—Cut common 3 × 4 scantling two feet longer than you wish your highest story to be; set up a double row, with the lower end resting firmly upon the edge of the hardened cement in the bottom of the trench; range them true and "plumb" them, letting them stand three or four inches farther apart than you desire your wall to be in thickness; then nail cleats across, above and below, to keep them in place, adding also "stays" or "braces," driven slantingly into the ground and nailed to the scantling at the upper end. Your skeleton or frame-work of scantling being all set up and "stayed" firm and "plumb," proceed to arrange your "boxing" for holding the concrete, and keeping the walls in shape. This is done by cutting sound inch or inch-and-a-half plank of ten inches or a foot wide, so as to fit inside of the two rows of scantling and form two sides of a box. Movable pieces the thickness of the wall are dropped in between, at intervals, to keep the box of the proper width, and wedges driven in between the boxing and the scantling, on the outside, prevent spreading by the pressure of the concrete. Wooden "clamps," to slip down, here and there, over the upper edges of the boxing, will also be found very serviceable.

5. *Mixing Concrete, Laying up, etc.*—It will be well to have at least four large mortar beds, one on each side of the house, made of strong plank, in the usual way. These should be surrounded by casks of water (oil casks cut in two are excellent), piles of rock, sand, gravel, etc.—the lime, of course, to be kept under cover, and used as wanted. Slack up your lime until it forms a thin, smooth, creamy mass, then add four or five parts of clean, sharp sand, stirring and mixing constantly, and using water enough to bring the whole, when thoroughly mingled, to the consistency of a thick batter. Into this "batter" mix coarse and fine gravel (that has previously been screened) until the mass is thick enough to be lifted on a common shovel. [The proper and

---

lime"—*not* the cement, which is, also, often called "hydraulic." It may be obtained from the quarry of Rev. C. W. Howard, Kingston, Cass County, Ga. But good common lime will answer, where the "hydraulic" can not be had.

thorough mixing of the sand with the lime, and the gravel with the mortar afterward, is very important, and should only be intrusted to your most careful hands.] Having one or two "beds" full of this mixture, you are ready to begin your wall. Wheel the mortar to the foundation in common railroad wheelbarrows, letting the common hands shovel it into the bottom of the trenches, while the superintendent or "boss" workman spreads it evenly with his trowel. When the bottom layer of mortar, three inches thick, is laid in, wheel large and small rock (previously sprinkled with water) to the wall, and press it into the soft mortar at every available point, leaving a small space between each piece of rock, and working the soft mortar against the plank boxing, to preserve a smooth surface on the wall. When you can press no more rock into the mortar, pour another layer of the latter over and through the rock, then add a layer of rock, as before, and so on, until your boxing all around is full. You have now ten inches or a foot of wall, all around, built; and if the lime is good and the weather dry, it will be hard enough in twenty-four hours to raise your boxes another tier. This is readily done by knocking out the wedges between the plank and the scantling, raising up the plank and sustaining it in place by "cleats" nailed on the scantling. In raising the boxing, begin at the point where you commenced laying up the day previous, as that portion of the wall will, of course, be the hardest. It is not necessary to raise *all* the boxing at once, or go entirely around the wall in a day. A foot or yard of the wall can be completed at a time, if advisable; but if the complete round can be made, so much the better. Planks to cover up with, in case of a sudden shower, or when a storm is apprehended, should be provided, and placed within reach.

6. *General Details, Floors, Windows, Doors, etc.*—We prefer a cement floor for the basement, on many accounts; but those who desire a wooden floor should leave air-holes in the outer walls, under the lower floor, six inches above the surface. This may be easily done by inserting wedge-shaped blocks or pins through the wall, to be knocked out afterward. When you are ready to lay the floors, level up your walls and run one course of brick all around, the thickness of the wall, for the ends of the flooring-joists to rest on—filling in around these ends with concrete, when they are fixed in their proper places. The door and window frames should be made of three-inch yellow pine, the full thickness or width of the walls, and may be set up and built around, like those in a brick house, as the wall progresses. A piece of common inch plank, "cut in" all around them, to prevent the actual contact of the damp mortar, will keep them, in a great measure, from warping. Where base-boards are needed, blocks of scantling may be built in flush with the inner surface of the wall, at the proper distances apart.

H.

PRACTICAL HINTS BY A BUILDER.

1. *The Roof.*—No roof should project less than one foot—it may project as much as you like up to two feet.

Too often, at present, in the commoner kind of country houses, the roof-boards are cut off even with the sides and ends of the house, and the shingles allowed to project only *half an inch!* What happens? All the rain that falls upon it runs over the entire surface of the house, discoloring the paint and washing it away.

2. *Windows.*—There should be a bold projection over each window, instead of the single inch which the cap, so called, is now generally allowed to extend beyond the casing. The slight projection furnishes no protection to the sash, which is continually washed by the rain, and prematurely decays.

The casings or dressings of the windows are generally too narrow. They should never be less than three and a half inches, and may be wider if you like. Let the head or top piece be an inch and a half wider than the sides. One and a quarter inches is the proper thickness for all outside casings. For caps, one-and-three-fourth-inch plank (one-and-a-half-inch will do) should be used. They should be six inches wide. Reduce one edge to the thickness of an inch. Nail the cap upon the edge of the top casing, and against the frame of the house, and it will form a bold and efficient projection.

3. *Gutters.*—Let the ends of the rafters come out flush with the side of the frame. To these and to the plate are nailed the brackets, cut from one-and-a-quarter-inch stuff, which are to support the gutter. The brackets should project one foot, and be lined with inch boards for trimming. The outside must be covered with dressed stuff of the proper style. There must be a frieze or margin, running the entire length of the house, under the gutter, and also on the gable. It may vary in width, on different houses, from ten to twenty inches.—*A. Blauvelt.*

I.

SPECIFICATIONS FOR COTTAGE.

See Figs. 20, 21, 22, 23.

SIZE, HEIGHT, ETC.—For all dimensions and the general arrangement, reference is to be had to the plans and elevations (pp. 59–61). Cellar to be 5¾ feet high—3 feet below ground and 2¾ above. First floor to be 8 feet in height, clear, and the attic 7½ feet, clear, with 5½ feet breast-work.

DIGGING.—The digging includes the cellar, trenches for the foundations, and a water cistern 5 feet in diameter and 5 feet deep.

STONE WORK.—Trenches to be filled with good stone. Sills for cellar windows to be blue stone, 2 × 10 inches.

BRICK WORK.—Cellar and foundation walls to be 8 inches thick. The fire-places and the top of the chimney above the roof to be of hard brick laid up in good sharp sand and lime mortar. Walls of the cistern to be 4 inches thick, laid in cement, the sides and bottom to be well cemented.

PLASTERING.—All rooms, landings, and closets to be lathed, scratch-coated browned, and whitewashed.

TIMBER.—Sills to be 4 × 9; first tier of beams, 2 × 9; posts, 4 × 8; all to be of white pine. Enter-ties, 4 × 6 ; second tier of beams, 2 × 8 ; filling-in, studs, braces, and rafters, 3 × 4 ; all to be of hemlock. Cellar beams 1¼ × 4 spruce plank. Beams and rafters to be 2 feet from centers; studding, 16 inches from centers.

ROOFS.—To be lathed with 1¼ × 2 spruce strips, and covered with 2 feet cypress shingles, laid 7¼ inches to the weather.

INCLOSING.—To be done with pine boards ⅞ inch thick and about 8 inches wide, nailed horizontally to studs, with 1¼ inch lap.

PARTITIONS.—All partitions to be set with 2 × 4 hemlock strips, 16 inches from centers.

FURRING.—Hemlock furring strips to be used between the beams.

FLOORS.—These are to be laid with 1¼ inch mill-worked spruce plank.

STAIRS.—The stairs are to have 1¼ inch pine trees, 1¼ inch strings, and 1 inch risers, with plain, small balusters, and hand-rail of boxwood.

DOORS.—The doors for the first story to be 1¼ inch single-faced panel, and those of the attic to be 1¼ inch battened ; all to be well hung, and pro vided with rim locks, except the closet doors, which are to have catches.

WINDOWS.--To have the usual 1¼ inch plank frames, 1¼ inch sashes with improved catches, and to be glazed with plain American glass.

BLINDS.—All the windows to have plain Venetian blinds.

PAINTING.--Two coats of white lead or zinc paint to be put on to all the out side, and inside work generally painted.

GENERAL.—Inside doors and window casings to be 4½ inches wide, with back moldings to first story. Gu ters to be of tin (3½ inch) with proper leaders. For details of outside cornice, trimmings, porch, etc., consult a builder or architect.

J.

HOW TO BUILD BALLOON FRAMES.

The following is a report of some remarks made by Mr. Solon Robinson be fore the Farmers' Club of the American Institute, and first published in the New York *Tribune* of January 18th, 1855:

MR. ROBINSON said: At our last meeting I made some remarks, which were followed by others, upon the subject of "Balloon Frames" of dwellings and other public buildings, a slight sketch of which I published in *The Tribune*, not deeming it important to enter into the minutiæ of hours to make such buildings. I find that I did not appreciate the importance of the subject, for I have received a score of letters and personal inquiries from various parts of the country, showing that a great many farmers would like to know how to build a farm-house for half the present expense. I therefore ask the indulgence of the Club, while I start a balloon from the foundation and finish it to the roof. I would saw all my timber for a frame-house, or ordinary frame outbuilding, of the following dimensions: Two inches by eight; two by four two by one. I have, however, built them, when I lived on the Grand Prairie of Indiana, many miles from saw-mills, nearly all of split and hewed stuff, making use of rails or round poles, reduced to straight lines and even thickness on two sides, for studs and rafters. But sawed stuff is much the easiest, though in a timber-country the other is far the cheapest. First, level your foundation, and lay down two of the two-by-eight pieces, flatwise, for sidewalls. Upon these set the floor-sleepers, on edge, thirty-two inches apart. Fasten one at each end, and, perhaps, one or two in the middle, if the building is large, with a wooden pin. These end-sleepers are the end-sills. Now lay the floor, unless you design to have one that would be likely to be injured by the weather before you get the roof on. It is a great saving though, of labor, to begin at the bottom of a house and build up. In laying the floor first, you have no studs to cut and fit around, and can let your boards run out over the ends, just as it happens, and afterward saw them off smooth by the sill. Now set up a corner post, which is nothing but one of the two-by-four studs, fastening the bottom by four nails; make it plumb, and stay it each way. Set another at the other corner, and then mark off your door and window places, and set up the side studs and put in the frames. Fill up with studs between, sixteen inches apart, supporting the top by a line or strip of board from corner to corner, or stayed studs between. Now cover that side with rough sheeting boards, unless you intend to side-up with clap-boards on the studs, which I never would do, except for a small, common building. Make no calculation about the top of your studs; wait till you get up that high. You may use them of any length, with broken or stub-shot ends, no matter. When you have got this side boarded as high as you can reach, proceed to set up another. In the mean time, other workmen can be lathing the first side. When you have got the sides all up, fix upon the height of your upper floor, and strike a line upon the studs for the under side of the joist. Cut out a joist four inches wide, half-inch deep, and nail on firmly one of the inch strips. Upon these strips rest the chamber floor joist. Cut out a joist one inch deep, in the lower edge, and lock it on the strip, and nail each joist to each stud. Now lay this floor, and go on to build the upper story, as you did the lower one; splicing on and lengthening out studs wherever needed, until you get high enough for the plate. Splice studs or joist by simply butting the ends together, and nailing strips on each side. Strike a line and saw off the top of the studs even upon each side—not the ends—and nail on one of the inch-strips. That is the plate. Cut the ends of the upper joist the bevel of the pitch of the roof, and nail them fast to the plate, placing the end ones inside the studs, which you will let run up promiscuously, to be cut off by the rafter. Now lay the garret-floor by all means before you put on the roof, and you will find that you have saved fifty per cent. of hard labor. The rafters, if supported so as not to be over ten feet long, will be strong enough of the two by-four stuff. Bevel the ends and nail fast to the joist. Then there is no strain upon the sides by the weight of the roof, which may be covered with shingles or other materials—the cheapest being composition or cement roofs. To make one of this kind, take soft, spongy, thick paper, and tack it upon the boards in courses like shingles. Commence at the top with hot tar and saturate the paper, upon which sift evenly fine gravel, pressing it in while hot—that is, while tar and gravel are both hot. One coat will make a tight roof; two coats will make it more durable. Put up your partitions of stuff one by four, unless where you want to support the upper joist—then use stuff two by four, with strips nailed on top, for the joist to rest upon, fastening altogether by nails, wherever timbers touch. Thus you will have a frame without a tenon, or mortice, or brace, and yet it is far cheaper, and incalculably stronger when finished, than though it was composed of timbers ten inches square, with a thousand auger holes and a hundred days' work with the chisel and adze, making holes and pins to fill them.

To lay out and frame a building so that all its parts will come together, requires the skill of a master mechanic, and a host of men, and a deal of hard work to lift the great sticks of timber into position. To erect a balloon-building requires about as much mechanical skill as it does to build a board fence. Any farmer who is handy with the saw, iron square, and hammer, with one of his boys or a common laborer to assist him, can go to work and put up a frame for an outbuilding, and finish it off with his own labor, just as well as to hire a carpenter to score and hew great oak sticks and fill them full of mortices, all by the science of the "square rule." It is a waste of labor that we should all lend our aid to put a stop to. Besides, it will enable many a farmer to improve his place with new buildings, who, though he has long needed them, has shuddered at the thought of cutting down half of the best trees in his wood-lot, and then giving half a year's work to hauling it home, and paying for what I do know is the wholly useless labor of framing. If it had not been for the knowledge of balloon-frames, Chicago and San Francisco could never have arisen, as they did, from little villages to great cities in a single year. It is not alone city buildings, which are supported by one another, that may be thus erected, but those upon the open prairie, where the wind has a sweep from Mackinaw to the Mississippi, for there they are built, and stand as firm as any of the old frames of New England, with posts and beams sixteen inches square. These remarks were confirmed by the testimony of other members present, who testified to having adopted the mode of framing referred to with entire success.

K.

CISTERNS.

On this important subject we can not do better than copy the following article from the "Annual Register of Rural Affairs," for 1855 :

"The great value of an abundant supply of water to houses and barns, and which may be easily had by providing capacious cisterns, renders it important that the cheapest, best, and most convenient mode of construction should be adopted. The two all-essential requisites for underground cisterns are, good hydraulic lime and a supply of clear, pure sand. These must be selected from experience or trial, or by choosing such as have already proved efficient for this purpose. Good hydraulic cement will, in the course of a few months, become about as hard as sandstone.

"When this hardening process does not take place, it must be attributed to bad materials, or to intermixing in wrong proportions. On the latter point, some are misled by adopting the practice employed in mixing *common* lime mortar, the hardest material resulting in this case where the sand constitutes about five sixths of the whole. But the hardest *water-lime* mortar can not be made if the sand forms much more than two thirds of the whole.

Fig. 124.

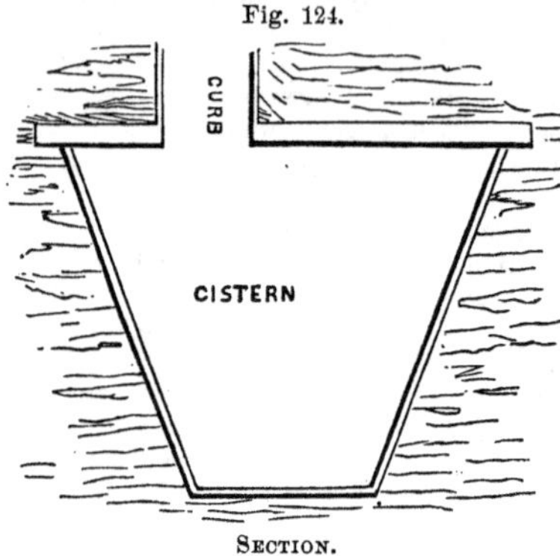

SECTION.

"A very common and cheap form for the cistern is, to dig a round hole into the ground with sloping sides, somewhat in the form of a narrow-bottomed tub, and then to plaster immediately upon the earth (fig. 124). Unless a slope is given to the sides, the mortar can not be made to keep its place while soft, as it is nearly impossible to find a soil dry and hard enough to retain the plastering by simple adhesion. The top of this kind of cistern must therefore be wide, and consequently difficult to cover very large ones effectually and substantially. The covering is usually made of stiff and durable plank, supported, if necessary, by strong scantling, and over this is placed about one foot of earth to exclude completely the frost. A hole with a curb about eighteen inches by two feet, must be left in this covering, for the admission of the water pipe or pump, and to allow a man to enter for cleaning out the cistern when necessary. In cold or freezing weather, it is indispensably requisite to have this hole stopped, to exclude frost, which would otherwise enter the wet cement or walls, and produce cracking or leakage—a frequent cause of the failure of water-lime cisterns.

Fig 125.

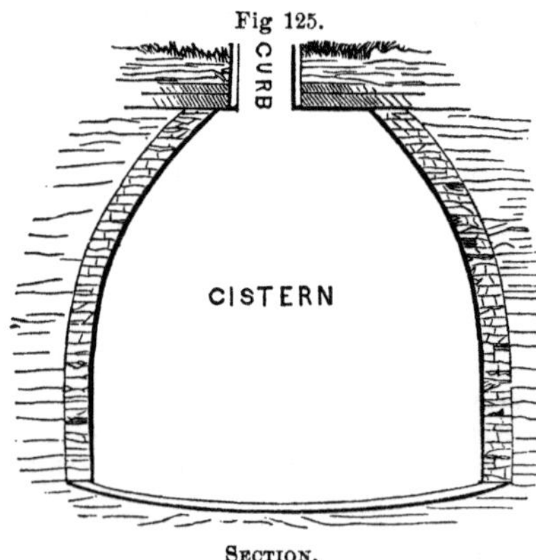

SECTION.

"This is the cheapest form of such reservoirs, but a better, more capacious and more durable mode, is to dig the hole with perpendicular sides in the form of a barrel, and build the walls with stone or brick, to receive the plastering (fig. 125). In consequence of its circular form, operating like an arch, these walls will not be in danger of falling if not more than half the ordinary thickness of similar walls. For large cisterns they should be thicker than for small ones. The walls should be built perpendicular until about half way up, when each successive layer should be contracted so as to bring them nearer together, in the form of an arch, reducing the size of the opening at the top, and rendering a smaller covering necessary. If the subsoil is always dry or never soaked or flooded with water, the walls may be laid in common lime mortar, and afterward plastered on the inner surface with the cement. But in wet subsoils, the whole wall should be laid in water lime. If the bottom is hard earth or compact gravel, a coating of an inch or two may be spread immediately upon the earth bottom; but in other instances, the bottom should be first laid with flat stone, or paved with round ones, the cement spread upon these.

"The plastering upon the sloping earth-walls, as first described (fig. 124), should never be less than an inch thick, and if the earth is soft it should be more. On the stone or hard brick walls (fig. 125), half an inch will be thick enough. Cisterns can rarely, if ever, be made free from leaking, without giving them at least two successive coats, and three will be safer—the previous coat in each instance being allowed to become dry and hard."

A filtering cistern may be made as follows:

"Make a partition (*a*) in the cistern, dividing it into two portions. This partition is pierced at the bottom with several apertures. A low wall (*b*) is built up on each side the partition, and a few inches above the top of the apertures.

Fig. 126.

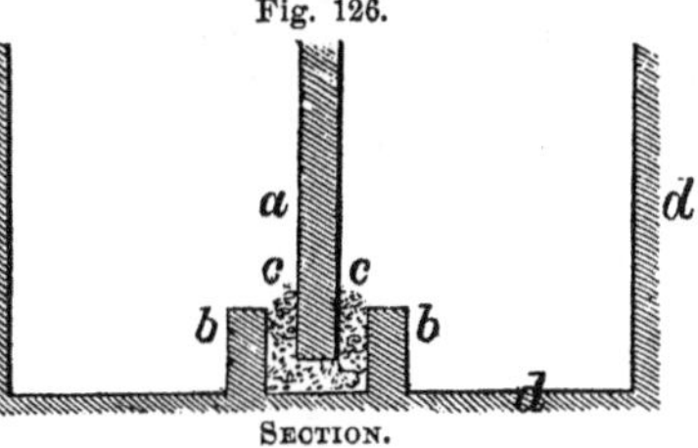

SECTION.

"The open space between these low walls (*c*) is filled with charcoal broken fine, and with gravel—the latter being on top. The water is conducted into one apartment, and may always be drawn up bright and clear from the other. The accompanying section, to which the letters have reference, may help to make this account more intelligible."*

Another plan is thus described by the same writer:

"A cask holding perhaps a hundred gallons is placed by the side of the larger cistern, and quite near the surface of the ground. An aperture in its bottom, over which is secured a large sponge, is connected by a good-sized pipe of wood or clay with the main tank. A third part of the cask is now filled with the charcoal and gravel; the conductor from the house is led into it, and the thing is complete.

---

* Village and Farm Cottages.

"This mode is not only as easy and as cheap as the other, but has this great advantage, that the filterer can be often and readily cleaned, while in the other case, it is necessary to remove all the water and to go down deep in order to accomplish the work."

L.

A CHEAP ICE-ROOM.

A farmer communicates the following in *Life Illustrated:*

"I send you my experience. I partitioned off the northeast corner of my wood-house, which opens to the west, and is 25 feet wide. The ice-room is about nine feet square; is clap-boarded on the studs on the north and east, and lined on the inside, leaving the four-inch space between empty. On the south is an inch-board partition, just tight enough to hold saw-dust. On the west I slip in boards like bars, any height I wish to pile my ice, and leave the upper part open, just as is convenient. This is my house.

"Into it, on the ground, I put from six to ten inches of saw-dust, then put in my ice one foot from the partition on every side, packing it in as closely as I can, and in as large blocks as I can conveniently handle. I then fill the spaces next the partitions with saw-dust, and a good depth (say one foot) over the top, and it is done for the year.

"I have practiced in this way two years past, and had all I wanted for dairy and other uses, and to give to my neighbors.

"The whole cost of making is 800 feet of hemlock boards, a few nails, and a half a day's work. Neighbor farmers, try it. Almost any other location is as good as this."

INDEX.

AMERICAN PHRENOLOGICAL JOURNAL.

A Repository of Science, Literature, and General Intelligence; Devoted to Phrenology, Physiology, Education, Mechanism, Agriculture, and to all those Progressive Measures which are calculated to Reform, Elevate, and Improve Mankind. Illustrated with Numerous Portraits and other Engravings. Quarto form, suitable for binding. Published Monthly, at One Dollar a Year.

It may be termed the standard authority in all matters pertaining to Phrenology, while the beautiful typography of the Journal, and the superior character of the numerous illustrations, are not exceeded in any work with which we are acquainted.—*Am. Cour.*

COMBE'S LECTURES ON PHRENOLOGY;

Including its appplication to the present and prospective condition of the United States. With Notes, an Essay on the Phrenological Mode of Investigation, and an Historical Sketch. By Andrew Boardman, M.D. Illustrated. Muslin, $1 25.

EDUCATION COMPLETE. Embracing

Physiology Animal and Mental, applied to the Preservation and Restoration of Health of Body and Power of Mind; Self Culture and Perfection of Character, including the Management of Youth; Memory and Intellectual Improvement, applied to Self Education and Juvenile Instruction. By Fowler. In 1 vol., $2 50.

Every one should read it who would preserve or restore his health, develop his mind and improve his character.

EDUCATION: Its Elementary Principles

founded on the Nature of Man. By J. G. Spurzheim, M. D. With an Appendix, containing a Description of the Temperaments, and an Analysis of the Phrenological Faculties. Price, in Paper, 62 cents. Muslin, 87 cents.

We regard this volume as one of the most important that has been offered to the public for many years. It is full of sound doctrines and practical wisdom.—*Boston Medical and Surgical Journal.*

MARRIAGE: Its History and Philoso-

PHY. With a Phrenological and Physiological Exposition of the Functions and Qualifications necessary for Happy Marriages. By L. N. Fowler. Illustrated. Paper, 50 cents; Muslin, 75 cents.

It contains a full account of the marriage forms and ceremonies of all nations and tribes, from the earliest history down to the present time. Those who have not yet entered into matrimonial relations, should read this book, and all may profit by a perusal. —*N. Y. Illustrated Magazine.*

SELF-CULTURE, AND PERFECTION OF

CHARACTER; including the Education and Management of Youth, By O. S. Fowler. Price, paper, 62 cents; Muslin, 87 cents.

"SELF-MADE, OR NEVER MADE," is the motto. No individual can read a page of it without being improved thereby. With this work, in connection with PHYSIOLOGY ANIMAL AND MENTAL, AND MEMORY AND INTELLECTUAL IMPROVEMENT, we may become fully acquainted with ourselves, comprehending, as they do, the whole man. We advise all to read these works.—*Com. School Advocate.*

PHRENOLOGICAL BUST; designed especially for learners. Showing the Exact Location of all the Organs of the Brain. Price, including box for packing, $1 25. [By Express. Not mailable.]

This is one of the most ingenious inventions of the age. A cast made of plaster of Paris, the size of the human head, on which the exact location of each of the phrenological organs is represented, fully developed, with all the divisions and classifications. Those who cannot obtain the services of a professor, may learn in a very short time, from this model head, the science of Phrenology, so far as the location of the organs is concerned.—*N. Y. Sun.*

MEMORY AND INTELLECTUAL IMPROVEMENT; applied to Self-Education and Juvenile Instruction. By O. S. Fowler. Enlarged and Improved. Illustrated. Paper, 62 cents; Muslin, 87 cents.

The science of Phrenology, now so well established, affords us important aid in developing the human mind, according to the laws of our being. This, the work before us is preëminently calculated to promote, and we cordially recommend it to all.—*Dem. Rev.*

SELF-INSTRUCTOR IN PHRENOLOGY AND PHYSIOLOGY. Illustrated with 100 Engravings; including a Chart for recording the various Degrees of Development. By O. S. and L. N. Fowler. Price, paper, 25 cents; muslin, 50 cents.

This treatise is emphatically a book for the million. It contains an explanation of each faculty, full enough to be clear, yet so short as not to weary; together with combinations of the faculties, and engravings to show the organs, large and small; thereby enabling all persons, with little study, to become acquainted with practical Phrenology.

FAMILIAR LESSONS ON PHRENOLOGY and PHYSIOLOGY; for Children and Youth. Two volumes in one. $1 25.

The natural language of each organ is illustrated, and the work is brought out in a style well adapted to the family circle, as well as the school-room.—*Teachers' Comp'n.*

MORAL AND INTELLECTUAL SCIENCE; applied to the Elevation of Society. By Combe, Cox, and others. $2 30.

This work contains Essays on Phrenology, as a department of physiological science, exhibiting its varied and important applications to social and moral philosophy, to legislation, medicine, and the arts. With Portraits of Drs. Gall, Spurzheim, and Combe.

MENTAL SCIENCE. Lectures on the Philosophy of Phrenology. By Rev. G. S. Weaver. Illustrated. 87 cents.

These Lectures were prepared for the intellectual, moral, and social benefit of society. The author has, in this respect, done a good work for the rising generation

DEFENCE OF PHRENOLOGY; containing the Nature and value of Phrenological Evidence. A work for doubters. 87 cents.

LOVE AND PARENTAGE; applied to the Improvement of Offspring; By O. S. Fowler. Price 30 cents.

LOVE AND PARENTAGE, AND AMATIVENESS; in one vol. Muslin, 75 cents.

RESULTS OF HYDROPATHY; OR, CON- STIPATION not a Disease of the Bowels; Indigestion not a Disease of the Stomach; with an Exposition of the true Nature and Causes of these Ailments, explaining the reason why they are so certainly cured by the Hydropathic Treatment. By Edward Johnson, M. D. Muslin. Price, 87 cents.

WATER-CURE LIBRARY. In Seven Vol- umes, 12mo. Embracing the most popular works on the subject. By American and European Authors. Bound in Embossed Muslin. Price, only $7 00.

This library comprises most of the important works on the subject of Hydropathy. The volumes are of uniform size and binding, and form a most valuable medical library.

WATER AND VEGETABLE DIET in Con- sumption, Scrofula, Cancer, Asthma, and other Chronic Diseases. In which the Advantages of Pure Water are particularly considered. By William Lambe, M. D., With Notes and Additions by Joel Shew, M. D. 12mo., 258 pp. Paper, 62 cents. Muslin, 87 cents.

ACCIDENTS AND EMERGENCIES: A Guide, containing Directions for Treatment in Bleeding, Cuts, Bruises, Sprains, Broken Bones, Dislocations, Railway and Steamboat Accidents, Burns and Scalds, Bites of Mad Dogs, Cholera, Injured Eyes, Choking, Poison, Fits, Sun-stroke, Lightning, Drowning, etc., etc. By Alfred Smee, F. R. S. Illustrated with numerous Engravings. Appendix by Dr. Trall. Price, prepaid, 15 cents.

PARENTS' GUIDE FOR THE TRANSMIS- SION of the Desired Qualities to Offspring; and Childbirth made Easy By Mrs. Hester Pendleton. Price, 60 cents

PREGNANCY AND CHILDBIRTH. Illus- trated with Cases, Showing the Remarkable Effects of Water in Mitigating the Pains and Perils of the Parturient State. By Dr. Shew. Paper. Price, 30 cents.

INTRODUCTION TO THE WATER-CURE. Founded in Nature, and adapted to the Wants of Man. Price, 15 cents.

SEXUAL DISEASES; their Causes, Pre- vention, and Cure, on Physiological Principles. Embracing Home Treatment for Sexual Abuses; Chronic Diseases, especially the Nervous Diseases of Women; The Philosophy of Generation; Amativeness; Hints on the Reproductive Organs. In one volume. Price, $1 25.

THE SCIENCE OF HUMAN LIFE. By Sylvester Graham, M.D. With a Portrait and Biography of the Author. $2 50.

CURIOSITIES OF COMMON WATER; or, the Advantages thereof in preventing and curing Diseases; gathered from the Writings of several Eminent Physicians, and also from more than Forty Years' Experience. By John Smith, C. M. With Additions, by Dr. Shew. 30 cents.

Miscellaneous.

HOW TO WRITE: a New Pocket Manual

of Composition and Letter-Writing, embracing Hints on Penmanship and choice of Writing Materials, Practical Rules for Literary Composition in general, and Epistolary and Newspaper Writing, Punctuation, and Proof Correcting in particular; Directions for Writing Letters of Business, Relationship, Friendship and Love, Illustrated with numerous Examples of Genuine Epistles from the pens of the Best Writers, to which are added Forms for Letters of Introduction, Notes, Cards, &c. Paper, 30 cents; muslin, 50 cents.

HOW TO TALK: a New Pocket Manual

of Conversation and Debate, with Directions for Acquiring a Grammatical and Graceful Style, embracing the Origin of Language, a Condensed History of the English Language, a Practical Exposition of the Parts of Speech, and their Modifications and Arrangement in Sentences; Hints on Pronunciation, the Art of Conversation, Debating, Reading and Books, with more than Five Hundred Errors in Speaking Corrected. Paper, 30 cents; muslin, 50 cents.

HOW TO BEHAVE: a New Pocket Manual

of Republican Etiquette, and Guide to Correct Personal Habits; embracing an Exposition of the Principles of Good Manners, Useful Hints on the Care of the Person, Eating, Drinking, Exercise, Habits, Dress, Self-Culture, and Behavior at Home; the Etiquette of Salutations, Introductions, Receptions, Visits, Dinners, Evening Parties, Conversation, Letters, Presents, Weddings, Funerals, the Street, the Church, Places of Amusement, Traveling, &c; with Illustrative Anecdotes, a Chapter on Love and Courtship, and Rules of Order for Debating Societies. Paper, 30 cents; muslin, 50 cents.

HOW TO DO BUSINESS: a New Pocket

Manual of Practical Affairs and Guide to Success in Life; embracing the Principle, of Business; Advice in Reference to a Business Education; Choice of a Pursuit, Buying and Selling, General Management, Manufacturing, Mechanical Trades, Farming, Book and Newspaper Publishing, Miscellaneous Enterprises, Causes of Success and Failure, How to Get Customers, Business Maxims, Letter to a Young Lawyer, Business Forms, Legal and Useful Information, and a Dictionary of Commercial Terms. Paper, 30 cents; muslin, 50 cents.

HAND BOOKS FOR HOME IMPROVEMENT

(Educational); comprising, "How to Write," "How to Talk," "How to Behave," and "How to Do Business," in one large gilt volume. Price, $1 50.

HOPES AND HELPS FOR THE YOUNG

of both Sexes; Relating to the Formation of Character, Choice of Avocation, Health, Amusement, Music, Conversation, Cultivation of Intellect, Moral Sentiments, Social Affection, Courtship and Marriage. By Rev. G. S. Weaver. Price, in paper, 62 cents; muslin, 87 cents.

HINTS TOWARDS REFORMS; consisting of Lectures, Essays, Addresses, and other Writings. With the Crystal Palace and its Lessons. Second Edition, Enlarged. By Horace Greeley. Price, $1 25.

HUMAN RIGHTS, AND THEIR POLITI- cal guarantees. By Hurlbut. With Notes, by Combe. Paper, 62 cts.; muslin, 87 cts.

NATURAL LAWS OF MAN. A Philo- sophical Catechism. By J. G. Spurzheim, M. D. An important work. 30 cents.

HOME FOR ALL. A New, Cheap, Con- venient and Superior Mode of Building; containing Full Directions for Constructing Gravel Walls. With Views, Plans and Engraved Illustrations. Price, 87 cents.

DEMANDS OF THE AGE ON COLLEGES. A Speech Delivered by Hon. Horace Mann, President of Antioch College. With an Address to the Students on College Honor. Price, 25 cents.

AIMS AND AIDS FOR GIRLS AND YOUNG WOMEN, on the various duties of life, including Physical, Intellectual, and Moral Development; Self-Culture Improvement, Education, the Home Relations, their Duties to Young Men, Marriage, Womanhood, and Happiness. By Rev. G. S. Weaver. Paper, 62 cts.; muslin, 87 cts.

SCIENCE OF SWIMMING. Giving a History of Swimming, and Instructions to Learners. By an Experienced Swimmer. Illustrated with Engravings. 15 cents. Every boy should have a copy.

WAYS OF LIFE: or, the Right Way AND THE WRONG WAY. A First Rate Book for all Young People. By Rev. G. S. Weaver. Paper, 50 cts.; muslin, 60 cts.

DELIA'S DOCTORS: or, a Glance Behind the Scenes. By Hannah Gardner Creamer. Paper, price 62 cents; muslin 87 cents.

IMMORTALITY TRIUMPHANT. The Ex- istence of a God and Human Immortality, Practically Considered, and the Truth of Divine Revelation Substantiated. By Rev. John Bovee Dods. Muslin, 87 cts

KANZAS REGION: Embracing Descrip- tions of Scenery, Climate, Productions, Soil, and Resources of the Territory. Interspersed with Incidents of Travel. By Max Greene. Price 30 cts; mus. 50 cts.

www.ingramcontent.com/pod-product-compliance
Lightning Source LLC
LaVergne TN
LVHW011226110826
845150LV00006B/1562

* 9 7 8 1 4 2 5 5 1 5 0 9 6 *